THY ROD and THY STAFF
They Comfort Me

BOOK III

A Biblical Study on
Maternal Intuition
and its link to the
Issue of Spanking Children

SAMUEL MARTIN

Recompense to no man evil for evil. Provide things honest in the sight of all men.

If it be possible, as much as lieth in you, live peaceably with all men.

Dearly beloved, avenge not yourselves, but rather give place unto wrath:

for it is written, Vengeance is mine; I will repay, saith the Lord.

Therefore if thine enemy hunger, feed him; if he thirst, give him drink:

for in so doing thou shalt heap coals of fire on his head.

Be not overcome of evil, but overcome evil with good. - Romans 12:17-21

© Copyright 2020 by Samuel Martin

Cover design and interior formatting by Dara Stoltzfus

First Edition – Fall 2020

Samuel Martin
Email: info@biblechild.com
Website: www.biblechild.com

ISBN: 9780978533939

All rights reserved. Except for brief excerpts for review purposes, no part of this book may be reproduced or used in any form or by any means – electronic or mechanical, including photocopying, recording, or information storage and retrieval systems – without the written permission from the copyright owner.

This volume is dedicated to the 100's of sisters in Christ who have supported me since the publication of the first edition of my book, *Thy Rod and Thy Staff, They Comfort Me: Christians and the Spanking Controversy*, published in 2006.

TABLE OF CONTENTS

Introduction 6
"Thy Rod and Thy Staff, They Comfort Me – Book III –
A biblical study on maternal intuition and its link to the issue of spanking children"

Chapter 1 7
Troubling messages reaching hearts/minds of many Christian mothers from well-intentioned but mistaken Christian religious leaders/authority figures

Chapter 2 13
Before elevating our minds to heavenly places,
we must unpack this teaching here on Earth

Chapter 3 17
The heart is not always all that bad

Chapter 4 24
Understanding the "soul" and its relation to the "heart" in the Bible

Chapter 5 29
"The heart" in the Bible can also mean 'mind', 'inner man', 'will' or 'understanding'

Chapter 6 39
"Gut Feelings: Does the Bible speak about them?"

Chapter 7 49
Mothers – You Are Fearfully and Wonderfully Made

Chapter 8 52
"A lesson about Intuition from a Mother Ostrich"

Chapter 9 57
"the one who believes in me will also do the works that I do and, in fact, will do greater works than these"

Chapter 10 61
In their own words – Christian mothers speak about intuition
A Plea to Mothers - A Guest Post by Heather Schopp
Mothers - Follow Your Instincts - A Guest Post by Debbie Davison

Appendix I 77
The Bear Mother and the Sacrifice of Jesus Christ

Other books by Samuel Martin 88
- Testimonies from Christian moms about the book Thy Rod and Thy Staff, They Comfort Me: Christians and the Spanking Controversy
- About the Author

INTRODUCTION

Thy Rod and Thy Staff They Comfort Me – Book III
A biblical study on the subject of maternal intuition and its link to the issue of spanking children

Since my book *"Thy Rod and Thy Staff, They Comfort Me: Christians and the Spanking Controversy"* (2006)[1] came out, I have connected and dialogued with 100s of Christian mothers. I have learned so much from these exchanges. I remain constantly in awe. The things I have learned changed me. The wisdom, knowledge and understanding I have received from Christian mothers who I know is supernatural. They are incredibly deep thinkers and profound students of God's Word. Their experience as mothers offers us a glimpse into God's mind. He endowed women with supernatural gifts to help them care for their children based on His design. God speaks to and through His daughters and many of us have not been listening properly. Today, this is changing.

The holy information I continue to learn forces me to ask hard questions, to raise the bar of understanding higher, to open up more complex topics for discussion and consideration. The subject of maternal intuition and its link to spanking children is an important topic to discuss, exchange information on and learn more about. This is the goal of this book. Having fearless thinkers around to challenge me is such a treasure. Continually asking hard and good questions is the first step to good answers being more possible. "Say to wisdom, "You are my sister," … (Proverbs 7:4 ESV)

Samuel Martin – Jerusalem, Fall 2020

---

[1] Available for free download from my website - http://www.biblechild.com/assets/thy-rod-and-thy-staff-they-comfort-me-mar-2013.pdf

1

Troubling messages reaching hearts/minds of many Christian mothers from well-intentioned but mistaken Christian religious leaders/authority figures

What is intuition? Is it real? I want to know what it is. I want to know how it works. I want to understand it. I want to know if it is something connected to the Spirit of God.

For me, writing about this subject is unfamiliar. It is uncomfortable. It is risky. But these are the precise reasons I feel I must write about intuition. Why? Because I want to learn more about this most powerful and beautiful gift that God has given to humanity and to understand it. This is where the beauty of information exchange allows for individual and collective knowledge to increase. Sharing knowledge and new ideas certainly promises to enrich the one sharing as well as those receiving. I believe we must embrace intuition, cultivate it and cherish it. This is what this book is all about.

I see my own wife, Sonia, using intuition. There are certain things she just knows. She definitely has a "mom brain" (thanks to PD) as I have heard it described. Her internal compass operates on a whole different orientation than does my own, especially if one of our two daughters is ill or something just doesn't feel right.

I have heard from scores of Christian mothers who have read my first book on spanking children.[2] Over and over again, these mothers have told me the book helped validate their own maternal instincts. Some even went to so far as to say that it transformed their inner lives. Many Christian mothers have told me they intuitively felt an internal feeling, an intuition, a leading, an inner voice, a gut feeling, a tugging feeling, a moral compass, telling them not to subject their children to corporal punishment (spanking/smacking). After hearing this message many times, I began to listen carefully

---

[2] Thy Rod and Thy Staff, They Comfort Me: Christians and the Spanking Controversy – Available free here – www.biblechild.com or on Amazon in hard copy - https://www.amazon.com/gp/product/0978533909/ref=dbs_a_def_rwt_bibl_vppi_i1

to this feedback. I really wanted to understand this idea more. It is a blessing to hear from Christian mothers about their intuition moving them toward peace and non-violence. It really seems that this "peace" is very much a Holy Spirit fruit. (Gal. 5:22,23)

Having said this, there is another side to this story that is less positive. The subject of intuition can disquiet Christian mothers. It can make them feel inferior, uncomfortable and disempowered. Why? Because intuition is often spoken of negatively from some pulpits. Many religious leaders believe they are helping women to follow God's Word by telling them to ignore, turn off, run from and never listen to these inner voices or leadings. These misguided religious leaders, though, often do not realize they can hurt (not help) Christian mothers and their families by their actions.

Why is this? Women are told they are inferior, imperfect or flawed. It is shocking to imagine such a message taught from a Christian pulpit, but it happens. It is so common and it negatively affects 1,000s of Christian women and mothers globally.

What are some Christian religious leaders and family members telling women?

My real interest in this subject began around 2010. A friend (CT) urged me to consider writing on the subject of women being told by ministers to ignore their intuitive feelings and never trust their inner voices and especially not their hearts. At that time, I acknowledged the need to write on this subject, but I did not follow through. I just was not ready to write on it. (When are men ever ready to write on maternal intuition?)

On the practical level, this subject is simple. It is saying to Christian women and mothers that you are flawed. You need to recognize that fact. To remedy this negative situation, you need to listen to the male Christian religious leaders in your lives starting with your husbands and there is no exception when this is not the case.

We also find that first time Christian mothers, who are much more sensitive to these maternal leadings, are told to turn these feelings off and ignore them. Often they are told these intuitive feelings are evil, wrong and not from God. They are told: "Do not listen to, nurture, feel, be sensitive to or heed the call of your child. Listen to your husband, fathers, elder male relatives and definitely your pastor and other male religious leaders first and foremost." Dozens of written resources and books exist talking about how Christian women should parent and raise their children and more often than not these books are written by men. In addition, in some cases, we often find some elder women reinforcing and reiterating these messages against the cultivation of intuition.

Many Christian women are being told that they are wrong on all counts when it comes to their motherly inner voices and leadings which guide them. Here is where the Bible is introduced and used in an aggressive and dogmatic way to reinforce this idea.

The Bible texts often used to promote this teaching are so familiar to Christian women and mothers. They are reinforced and drilled into the heads of Christian women of all ages over and over again. Here are some of the main ones:

"The heart is deceitful above all things, and desperately sick; who can understand it?" (Jeremiah 17:9 ESV)

In addition to this text, we must add:

"But what comes out of the mouth proceeds from the heart, and this defiles a person. For out of the heart come evil thoughts, murder, adultery, sexual immorality, theft, false witness, slander. These are what defile a person. …" (Matthew 15:18-20 ESV)

Many Christian women are told that their hearts, minds and souls are evil, not to be trusted or engaged and especially not listened to or ever heeded in any way. On the contrary, Christian women are told to run from, suppress or ignore these evil feelings.

This text is also used to reinforce this idea:

"For I know that nothing good dwells in me, that is, in my flesh." (Romans 7:18 ESV)

This text is also used in this same line of thinking:

"But Jesus on his part did not entrust himself to them, because he knew all people and needed no one to bear witness about man, for he himself knew what was in man." (John 2:24-25 ESV)

When one interprets these texts in light of maternal intuition or maternal instincts, this can cause massive confusion especially in the hearts and souls of dear sisters in Christ. This is especially true for a new mother. New mothers are particularly susceptible to allowing someone to influence their intuitive feelings toward the positive or the negative depending on the circle of people in their lives. Of course, the God's Word is a powerful force (as it should be if used rightly), which is often used to control these natural intuitive feelings/inclinations and is often swiftly used by male authority figures and notably pastors to head off the development and nurturing of these feelings.

In other words, Christian mom who loves God and His Word, just turn off your soul and your intuition and let us men tell you how to be, to act, to think, to feel and to keep you on the straight and narrow so you don't feel any worse than you have already been made to feel with the basic idea that comes from this teaching. Christian men in general are telling believing women: We know what is best. We are the authority figures. We are here to guide you and tell you what God wants you to do or not to do.

Add to this, the fact that you are never, ever under any circumstance ever to listen to your inner voices or intuitive feelings. By no means ever, if you wish to be on God's side. Note how this teaching is taught using the following text:

"Trust in the LORD with all your heart, and do not lean on your own understanding. In all your ways acknowledge him, and he will make straight your paths. Be not wise in your own eyes; fear the LORD, and turn away from evil." (Proverbs 3:5-7 ESV)

Look at how such a text could be used against maternal intuition. Not only could this text be used, IT IS BEING USED, or should I say MISUSED in the name of God.

To further alienate women from the God who created them perfect just as they are, an additional reminder of how different and beneath God we humans are is found in this text. However, in a patriarchal system, this text succeeds in letting women under these systems know that all thinking is just off limits and best left to exclusively to men or people who are older or in authority positions in churches. Note this text:

"For my thoughts are not your thoughts, neither are your ways my ways, declares the LORD. For as the heavens are higher than the earth, so are my ways higher than your ways and my thoughts than your thoughts." (Isaiah 55:8-9 ESV)

Add in all the theology and negative teachings that the Church has given about women and the superiority that men have and it just further compounds a terrible error.

I think we can all see that depending on how these texts are interpreted and in whose hands the interpretation is being given, they can be very harmful to dear sisters in Christ seeking to do God's will and, unfortunately, they have been used in this fashion to great detriment. But does this need to be so? The answer is NO!

Male authority figures tell Holy Spirit filled Christian women how to be moms?

Now, if it was not bad enough that some male ministers take it upon themselves to tell women in their church communities how to think, feel and be, this destructive instruction even extends into the realm of child rearing. Many of us have heard about some of the books on child rearing, which teach mothers' principles like "Cry It Out" and definitely teach against things like co-sleeping urging mothers to keep their distance from their children. To these ideas, we add corporal punishment/spanking/smacking.

The church that I grew up in had one of these child training manuals, which was designed to help families understand the Word of God. Yes, male ministers wrote it and it featured all of the teachings we are here referencing. It was also a manual teaching parents to spank/smack and to do so aggressively even on very small children.

All of this to Christian mothers is often crazy making nonsense. They have almost no ability to change or challenge it. This is because of the almost seemingly all-powerful system of Christian religious patriarchy. Women are often just simply unable to question any male religious authority. The power that many male religious leaders often wield is all encompassing. So, the end result is: mothers are told to deny their motherly feelings and intuitions and just turn the mothering switch created by God down deep in their souls off and to keep it turned off no matter what. All the while, the whole reality, just feels so wrong, and many Christian women have no way to live differently. The chances to embrace intuition in such systems are few and far between.

Can we all see how potentially destructive to the souls of especially our dear sisters in Christ these horrible teaching are? What kind of messages are our beloved Christian mothers and sisters hearing from pulpits? In Christian books? From family members or others holding positions of influence over them? Here are some of the specific negative messages that I have heard communicated to me over the years.

1. You are flawed
2. You are dirty and need to be cleaned up
3. Your heart is full of evil and needs to be ignored and suppressed
4. There is nothing good inside of you
5. You cannot trust yourself and your God given intuition and maternal leadings
6. You are "too sensitive" (JCH) and that is bad
7. What you think you "just know" (AH) is wrong and almost certainly not from God
8. Do not ever trust your feelings. They are wrong and against God. If you listen to your own feelings, you will be embracing evil

To be clear on what I think about these teachings, I will quote a scholarly friend of mine, Professor William Webb. He has coined the phrase which really describes these teachings well. They are "***gutter theology***."

What needs to take place now, is to leave these misunderstandings in the gutter where they belong and to elevate our minds and souls to heavenly places (Colossians 3:1), where:

> *"I will bless the LORD who advises me; yes, at night my innermost being instructs me."*
> *(*Psalm 16:7 LEB*)*

2

Before elevating our minds to heavenly places, we must unpack this teaching here on Earth

How do we really begin in really unpacking this false teaching? Should women and mothers deny or ignore their internal maternal feelings? Should they subject these feelings to the control and supervision of their husbands, fathers and other male church leaders? In doing this, we need to attempt to reorient ourselves. We need a more truthful, fact and Scripture based approach to the question of these maternal intuitions. They are so real for many, but have been hidden due to wrong Bible teaching about the need for women to deny their God-given intuition, internal compasses and instincts.

To do this, we have to first, I think, begin with a reasonable definition of what we are here talking about concerning maternal instinct or mother's intuition. I had have a chance to talk to a few close friends (who are Christian mothers) and I am going to suggest this formulation taken directly from **Hasting's Encyclopedia of Religion and Ethics** (vol. 7, p. 397) found under the article "Intuitionalism" saying the following:

"The term 'intuition' (Latin, *intueri* – to look upon) symbolizes the conception that one among the sources of knowledge is the direct and immediate apprehension of truth."

It is important here to touch on the meaning of 'apprehension' here because what it means is important. It means exactly "grasp" or "understanding".

When I speak to my Christian mother friends, this is the definition that I think really captures what it is they are telling me. Mother's intuition is a source of knowledge that gives the possessor of it a "direct and immediate understanding of truth."

As an example, my friend Lelia Schott (a mother of six from South Africa) describes it so eloquently saying:

"If I was hanging washing or something I would just get an ache in my chest or a feeling to check on baby and sure enough he/she would be rooting for milk." (rooting here means a reflex whereby babies open their mouths and move their heads and search for their mother's breast to feed – Quoted from Marianne Littejohn, an independent midwife from South Africa.)

Lelia further elaborates her feelings on this issue saying:

"Mother's Intuition is heart to heart communication - divine understanding within those nurturing immature life and love. I believe intuition is a gift mom's possess in order to fulfill the many emotional and physical needs of their young. To instinctively understand the whispers of a little heart entrusted to you is especially helpful as children are not always capable of expressing or protecting themselves."

Another friend Amanda Hughes (a mother of seven children) describes it like this:

"My personal view is the Holy Spirit within us telling us what we need to know. It is something that leads you to take a variety of different actions depending on the intensity of the "leading". ... The general crunchy community would say it is the natural knowing every woman knows. How to birth, how to nurse, how to nurture and care. ... The thought that God would leave a mother without guidance is just heartless. Labor and delivery is so hard. But I always knew I was safe. It is hard to feel safe while in intense pain. That is not a logical connection. Or if you YouTube "breast crawl" you can see babies crawl to the breast after being placed on a mother's abdomen. Logic would tell you that a baby cannot do that, or would not do that. But you can watch it happen. They have a knowing. Or a mom knowing when a baby is hungry, has to burp, or needs a diaper change. We know."

Amanda further comments: "I have felt God's peace with me in each of my child births. I have always been educated about childbirth, so I knew about it, but while enduring it you cannot think but just experience it through God's guidance. My body was orchestrating birth each time under God's conductorship. I knew God's hand was on my baby helping him or her navigate my body. That was actually the image I had in my head as I endured my labor pains, so it was comforting in my time of pain. This is the first big showing of a mother's intuition. The next is a mother comforting, feeding and tending to their newborn. Nobody has to tell a mother to do that, yet God guides, and science can confirm through the study of the hormone cascade. Since my first child, I always sought God in giving me direction as to what to do in my parenting. My first child was colicky and cried all the time. I was a mombie and when you cannot over analyze because you are exhausted, so you do what God gives you the wisdom to do. I never let her cry alone. I may not have known why she was upset, but I would meet her needs and then just be with her as she was upset. I hold onto the promise that my Abba Father will never leave me nor forsake me, so I can follow that model in how I parent. I need God to help me because I believe He is the Father to the fatherless. He understands when I do not. I often feel that I don't have all the answers, but I serve a God that does."

Jessica Claire Hall (a mother of three children) mentioned this as well:

"I've always been told that I'm "too sensitive." I've always had what I consider unique feelings and intuitions when it came to children."

In talking further, with several other mothers, we came up with the idea of what I might refer to as a kind of "positive leading" that mothers experience in particular relation to their children. I had some good general agreement on this from quite a number of Christian mothers that I know fairly well.

In addition to this though, I would like to add on what I think is an additional thought which gets back a little bit to our original definition of intuition and in this case we are here talking about mother's intuition. The key concept that is an important one for me is the idea that what we are here really describing is something where a spiritual experience takes place in the person of a mother and that experience leads her to grasp or understand the truth about something (generally [but not exclusively] connected to her children), which she could not otherwise have apprehended, known or understood.

Now, the importance of this point cannot be minimalized and here we are going to focus on the idea of the fact that through mother's intuition, mothers understand a truth or the truth about something and with repeated experience and cultivation, that truth is a truth that they can rely on and come to trust.

Now, how can we really know that this mother's intuition (or this "understanding of truth") is really a gift from God and is not something to be turned off or repressed like so many of our dear misguided male pastors/authority figures are telling our dear sisters in Christ? The reason for this is because the Bible teaches us that this "understanding" that mothers have is something that has been given them directly by God. We will look at how this teaching is given in Scripture.

Before we can do this properly, though, we really need first to make ourselves clear on what the Bible is talking about and what it means when it is speaking about the "heart", "soul", "mind" and "inner most parts" of a person. We really first need to properly understand these terms and their Biblical meanings before we can really begin to better comprehend this God-given gift of mother's intuition.

3

The heart is not always all that bad

One of the key texts used to disempower Christian women and moms and disconnect them from their intuitive guides is the following one found in Jeremiah 17:9:

"The heart is deceitful above all things, and desperately sick; who can understand it? (Jeremiah 17:9 ESV)

Now, to really understand this text, we need to undertake a deeper examination of the whole matter of the heart itself as we find the Scripture speaking about this issue. When we do that, we are going to find that this issue is not an easy one to understand. There is a complexity and depth in the material to be discussed and considered before concluding anything on this issue. While this has to be considered a reasonable approach, we will not hide our heads in the sand about what our Lord Jesus in particular said about the heart and about what the Bible overall says about the "heart".

Here I want to refer extensively to a beautiful and comprehensive article from the Cyclopedia of Biblical, Theological and Ecclesiastical Literature (**CBTEL**) under the title "heart" (Vol. IV, pg. 114ff). I have really benefitted from this essential piece of scholarship and I am really crafting this first part of this examination largely based on this superb article. In this article, the author really captures the complexity of understanding what the Bible teaches us about the subject of the heart.

As I have mentioned here and most of us are familiar with, the Bible has some factual statements about the "heart" which we must pay attention to and which often occupy the central guide for interpreting this issue among religious leaders. Note the following quotation, which helps us to consider the disposition of the human heart.

"In opposition to the superficial doctrine which makes man to regard to morals an indifferent being, Scripture present to us the doctrine of the natural wickedness of the human heart, the יצר לב (Hebrew: *yetzer lehv*) ("*the intention of man's heart*" - Genesis 8:21 ESV), or, more completely, יצר מחשבות לבו (Hebrew: *yetzer mahghshehvot levo*) ("*intention of the thoughts of his heart*" - Genesis 6:5 ESV – compare I Chronicles 28:9), and considers sin as having penetrated the center of life, from whence it contaminates its whole course." (CBTEL, Vol. IV, pg. 116)

This fact of the disposition of the human heart cannot be ignored or removed from our discussion. Mankind has a "heart" problem. Note the words of the Lord Jesus continuing:

"How can ye, being evil, speak good things? For out of the abundance of the heart the mouth speaketh" (Matthew 12:34; compare Ecclesiastes 8:11; Psalm 73:7); and those things which come out of the heart defile the man (Matthew 15:18)." (*ibid.*)

There is no getting around these statements of our Lord Jesus. They are true and need to be taken into consideration carefully because they come from a divine source. Having said that, they must be interpreted in a redemptive and not in an isolated way. Continuing:

"The heart is described as "deceitful (or, more properly עקב [Hebrew: *akov*], *crooked*, the opposite of ישר [Hebrew: *yahshar*], *straight*) above all things, and desperately wicked" (Jeremiah 17:9); so that God alone can thoroughly sound the depths of its wickedness (compare I John 3:20). Hence, the prayer of Psalm 139:23.

"Search me, O God, and know my heart! Try me and know my thoughts!" (Psalm 139:23 ESV)

If we just stop there, the whole thing sounds quite hopeless. But where we humans are concerned, God provides a very hopeful way forward and overall God is oriented towards redemption, reconciliation and hope. The Bible is moving toward redemption.

"Man, frightened at the manifestation of divine holiness, may take within himself the resolution of fulfilling the divine commands (Deuteronomy 5:24[3]); yet the divine voice complains (Deuteronomy 5:29) 'Oh that there were such a heart in them that they would fear (meaning to respect and show reverence towards) me!' etc. Therefore, the whole Revelation has for its object to change the heart of man; and its whole aim is to destroy, by virtue of its divine efficacy, the insusceptibility and the antagonism of the heart, and to substitute for them the fear of God in the heart (Jeremiah 32:40 – "I will make with them an everlasting covenant, that I will not turn away from doing good to them. And I will put the fear of me in their hearts, that they may not turn from me." ESV), so that the law may be admitted. (Jeremiah 31:33 and following[4])

This is where the hopefulness of the Bible's message really comes out:

"This is the effect of the operations of the Holy Spirit, whose workings, as shown in the Old Testament, point to the regeneration of the heart in redemption (Ezekiel 36:26 sq. 11:19), transforming the prophets into new creatures by means of a change of heart (I Samuel 10:6, 9), and implanting a willingness to obey God's law in the pious (Psalm 2:12-14)" (*ibid.* pg. 116)

---

[3] "And you said, 'Behold, the LORD our God has shown us his glory and greatness, and we have heard his voice out of the midst of the fire. This day we have seen God speak with man, and man still live." (Deuteronomy 5:24 ESV)

[4] "Behold, the days are coming, declares the LORD, when I will make a new covenant with the house of Israel and the house of Judah, not like the covenant that I made with their fathers on the day when I took them by the hand to bring them out of the land of Egypt, my covenant that they broke, though I was their husband, declares the LORD. For this is the covenant that I will make with the house of Israel after those days, declares the LORD: I will put my law within them, and I will write it on their hearts. And I will be their God, and they shall be my people. And no longer shall each one teach his neighbor and each his brother, saying, 'Know the LORD,' for they shall all know me, from the least of them to the greatest, declares the LORD. For I will forgive their iniquity, and I will remember their sin no more." (Jer. 31:31-34 ESV)

This is in summary the whole story of hope for the human heart summarized beautifully by the author of this article in CBTEL. It is this summary of hope that, unfortunately, we never hear about when it comes to the heart in humanity. We only seem to hear the negative side, especially directed towards Christian women and mothers telling them "don't trust your heart, it's always evil and wrong. End of story."

But this is not all that the Bible says about the "heart". It says quite a lot, but what it does really say requires study and the discussion is, in fact, quite complex. It is certainly not a subject to be understood by reviewing one or two Biblical texts and think that ends the matter. In no way! We really need to look at the whole counsel of God on this matter to see all aspects and teachings of what the Bible has to say about this most important subject. This will be the next step in this current examination.

To begin this extended and deep discussion, we have to preface this with the following overall understanding referring again to the excellent CBTEL article:

"In the Biblical point of view, human life, in all its operations, is centered in the heart. The heart is the central organ of the physical circulation; hence the necessity for strengthening the body as a support for the heart. (סעד לבך [Hebrew: *se'ad libbeka, refresh yourself*], Judges 19:5); and the exhaustion of physical power is called "a drying up of the heart." (Psalms 52:5; 22:15) (*ibid.* pg. 114.)

The heart has this physical side to it that we are all familiar with and the Bible is also familiar with this aspect of the heart and its role in the body, but the Bible also points to the more spiritual role that the "heart" plays in human life:

"So, also, is the heart the center of spiritual activity;" (*ibid.*)[5]

Continuing:

---

[5] Now, here I think it important, before moving on, to interject the important comment and fact that "spiritual activity" is something that takes place in the life of the Christian irrespective of gender! The Gospel of Jesus Christ and His Holy Spirit is given to men and women equally.

"for all spiritual aims, whether belonging to the intellectual, moral or pathological spheres, are elaborated in the heart, and again carried out by the heart." (*ibid.*)

Once again, we have to reiterate that this fact above applies both to men and women equally. Let's not miss this very important point because what we are going to see is that the intellectual, moral and pathological life of men and women, while both are human in orientation and divine in origin, at the same time, men and women are very different creatures, who are designed to go together in life, but each are indeed distinct beings with differences which have been made by God according to God's own design, for His Glory and according to His divine purposes. Continuing:

"In fact, the whole life of the soul, in the lower and sensual, as well as in the higher spheres, has its origin in the heart. (Proverbs 4:23, "*For out of it are the issues of life*")

This again is a very important quote because not only is the author speaking to women and men equally, so is the LORD, the one who inspired the writer of this section of the book of Proverbs to write those beautiful words.

But here the subject matter starts to get a little bit complex because we have to really carefully study the Bible to really differentiate some key issues concerning the matter of the "heart". This is especially the case concerning the need to differentiate between the "heart" and the "soul."

"In order to follow this train of thought, and to establish in a clearer light the Biblical view of the heart, it will be best to consider the relation the heart bears to the soul (Greek: ψυχή [*psuche*]; Hebrew נפש [*nephesh*]). This is one of the difficult questions in Biblical psychology." (*ibid.*)

That is correct. This is a very complex matter in the Holy Scripture. It takes a lot of study to elaborate these differences and really capture what the Bible is teaching us. Here we have to take great care to make sure we really have a studied understanding of these important questions, especially when it comes to issues where there are differences between the genders, which have been made by God by design. We don't want to have the wrong understanding and apply texts or information to one group wrongly and we certainly do not want to wrongly home in on just one isolated text (which today sadly is very commonplace) and develop a belief system just on that basis.

The words "heart" and "soul" are often used interchangeably in the Bible

The assertion that the words "heart" and "soul" in the Bible are often used interchangeably is made clear by a careful examination of a number of texts which it will pay us well to direct our attention to. For example, note the following:

In Deuteronomy 6:5 (compare Matthew 22:37; Mark 12:30, 33; Luke 10:27) and Deuteronomy 26:16, we are commanded to love God and obey his commandments with all our heart and all our soul (compare I Chronicles 28:9)" (*ibid.*) (See texts below)

"You shall love the LORD your God with all your **heart** and with all your **soul** and with all your might." (Deuteronomy 6:5 ESV)

"And he said to him, "You shall love the Lord your God with all your **heart** and with all your **soul** and with all your mind." (Matthew 22:37 ESV)

"And you shall love the Lord your God with all your **heart** and with all your **soul** and with all your mind and with all your strength.'(Mark 12:30 ESV); And to love him with all the **heart** and with all the understanding and with all the strength, and to love one's neighbor as oneself, is much more than all whole burnt offerings and sacrifices." (Mark 12:33 ESV)

"And he answered, "You shall love the Lord your God with all your **heart** and with all your **soul** and with all your strength and with all your mind, and your neighbor as yourself." (Luke 10:27 ESV)

"This day the LORD your God commands you to do these statutes and rules. You shall therefore be careful to do them with all your **heart** and with all your **soul**." (Deuteronomy 26:16 ESV)

"And you, Solomon my son, know the God of your father and serve him with a whole **heart** and with a willing mind, for the LORD searches all **hearts** and understands every plan and thought. ….". (1 Chronicles 28:9 ESV)

The same is the case in the following text from the book of Acts:

"Now the full number of those who believed were of one **heart**" … (Acts 4:32 ESV)

There are a number of other texts which are also relevant here. Note the following:

"In these passages, as in others, for instance, Deuteronomy 11:18, 30:2; Jeremiah 32:41, there is to be noticed, moreover, that the heart is always named first." (*ibid.*)

While this is indeed the case and there are these texts where we can notice some interchangeability with the words "heart" and "soul", in the vast majority of texts, this is not the case. This fact is documented by the following quotation.

"But in the majority of passages, where either the heart or the soul are separately spoken of, the term "heart" can either not be exchanged at all for the term "soul", or else only with some modification in the meaning." (*ibid*).

Now that we have a foundational understanding of the subject of the heart, we can now better consider the subject of the "soul" and its relation to the "heart" in the Bible.

4

Understanding the "soul" and its relation to the "heart" in the Bible

To further understand the Biblical teaching on this subject, we must look at the issue of the "soul" and the "fundamental distinction" (*ibid.*) between "heart" and "soul."

"The soul is the bearer of the personality (i.e. of the ego, the proper self) of man, in virtue of the indwelling spirit (Proverbs 20:27; I Corinthians 2:11), but yet is not itself the person of man;" (*ibid.*)

These are important and powerful texts, which need further discussion. Note them here:

"The spirit of man is the lamp of the LORD, searching all his innermost parts." (Proverbs 20:27 ESV)

"For who knows a person's thoughts except the spirit of that person, which is in him? So also no one comprehends the thoughts of God except the Spirit of God." (I Corinthians 2:11 ESV)

These are most important scriptures. There is a "spirit" in humanity. There is a spiritual side to human beings. But, this spiritual side takes time to develop! Human beings take time to develop and grow up. Children before the age of about five have an immaturely developed spirit. This is what is being taught in I Corinthians 2:11.

"At two and three he is a pig, groping in the garbage."[6]

The above description is a pretty good one. A two/three year old doesn't have an inner spirituality operating like an older child and certainly not like an adult! Not at all!

Human beings cannot know even the things of the "fleshly life" unless through the spirit, which is in man, as I Corinthians 2:11 teaches. This condition exists when a child is born and continues well into the time after age four or older. (depending on the individual) Some children after age four may begin to develop an inner personality.

By age five, children have some general awareness about life on a day to day basis (scientists who study this are aware of this fact), but prior to that time, they are certainly human, but the "*spirit of that person, which is in him*" has not yet developed and become aware of what it really means to be human. They have not developed a real personality or a self-awareness, as we adults know, understand and appreciate.

The heart, though, connected with the soul, plays a key role in the process of development of self:

"the heart, on the contrary, the 'חדרי בטן' [Hebrew: *chadre baten, all his inner most parts* (ESV)] of Proverbs 20:27, is the place where the process of self-consciousness is developed, in which the soul finds itself, and thus becomes conscious of its actions and impressions as its own ..." (CBTEL, vol. IV, pg. 114)

---

[6] Midrash (Koheles Rabbah 1:2) -- In the beginning of Koheles (Ecclesiastes), King Solomon seven times calls the physical world a place of "hevel" -- vanity or futility. The Midrash relates this to the seven stages of life. At one year of age, man is a king, fondled and doted upon by all. **At two and three he is a pig, groping in the garbage.** At ten he prances around like a kid. At twenty he is a horse, preening himself in search of a wife. After marriage he works like a donkey to earn a living. When he has children he is brazen as a dog trying to raise and support his family. And at the end of his life he becomes senile and senseless as an ape. A script few of us veer from. For better or worse -- as Yehuda wrote above -- life really is a mimicry of the animal kingdom!" (Here making reference to the ancient Hebrew book -- Pirke Avot - http://www.torah.org/learning/pirkei-avos/chapter5-25.html#)

However, in matters which concern a more comprehensive discussion about the whole human being, the soul, and not the heart, is found in key Biblical texts. Note this demonstrated quite clearly:

"Accordingly the soul, not the heart, is spoken of when the whole human being as such, and his physical or spiritual welfare or perdition [meaning the eternal destiny of an individual] are meant. This is seen on comparing such passages as Job 33:18, 22, 28: Psalm 44:17; and the expression of the New Testament περιποίισις ψυχης (Greek: *peripoyeesis psuche*) (Hebrews 10:39) ["*preserve their souls*" (ESV)]; ἀπολίσαι τὴν ψυχὴν (Greek: *apolisai ten psuchen*) ["*loses his life*" (ESV)] (Mark 8:35 compare Matthew 10:32; James 1:21)" (*ibid.*)

Several other texts to keep in mind in the same train of thought concerning the soul are:

"Take my yoke upon you, and learn from me, for I am gentle and lowly (meaning humble) in heart, and you will find rest for your souls." (Matthew 11:29 ESV)

"For what will it profit a man if he gains the whole world and forfeits his soul? Or what shall a man give in return for his soul?" (Matthew 16:26 ESV)

"Beloved, I urge you as sojourners and exiles to abstain from the passions of the flesh, which wage war against your soul." (1 Peter 2:11 ESV)

All of these texts have one important thing in common.

"In all of these passages it were impossible to substitute לב (*lehv*) or καρδία (*kardia*), ('heart' in Hebrew and Greek respectively) for נפש (*nephesh*) or ψυχή (*psuche*) ('soul' in Hebrew and Greek)" (ibid.)

This is why it is so important for us studying the subject of the heart and the soul (and especially so because what many religious leaders are teaching us [and especially our mothers] about these subjects.) There are important distinctions found in Scripture and we need to study the Bible carefully to see these important differences in meaning. Without such an examination, we may be on the path to a wrong understanding of God's message. This, unfortunately, is the present situation many find themselves in.

The same writer notes that:

"nor can we make the "*overseer of your souls*" (I Pet. 2:25 ESV) equivalent to the "*who know the hearts of all,*" (Acts 1:24 ESV) (*ibid.* – Note: English translation added by author)

Some of these discussions are somewhat technical when it comes to the variety of terms employed in the Biblical writers and herein is the important point. We need to know what we are talking about when it comes to this question of the heart and what it is we are being told the Bible teaches us about it. Today, this needs to happen more.

Notice how this is definitely the case in several passages from the books of Psalms and Jeremiah:

"neither can לבו (Hebrew: *lehvo, his heart*) be said of the יורדי עפר (Hebrew: *yordei gahphahr*) ("*who go down to the dust*" – Psalm 22:29 ESV)

חיה לבב (Hebrew: *chayah lehvahv*) ("*May your hearts live forever!*" - Psalm 22:26 ESV; "*let your hearts revive*" Psalm 69:32 ESV) has an essentially different meaning from חיתה נפש (Hebrew: *chaytah nephesh*) ("*your life shall be spared*" – Jer. 38:17, 20 ESV) (*ibid.*, pg. 115)

Another important example of the differences between the heart and the soul is found in this discussion by the same author:

"When Nabal lost consciousness in consequence of fear, his "soul" still dwelt in him (see Acts 20:10); but yet, according to I Samuel 25:37, his "heart" died within him. When fear suspends consciousness, the heart fails (Genesis 42:26)." (*ibid.*)

These are subtle differences between "heart" and "soul" which can be imperceptible if one does not follow the original languages carefully. Here we need to be very specific as well, because even depending on whether we are talking about humans or animals, the same term can be used to describe both. We are not, however, to understand that humans and animals have "souls" in the same sense even though the same terms to describe "living soul" or "living creature" may be used in a Biblical language (in Genesis 1:20 and 2:7, the same words in Hebrew נפש חיה [*nephesh chayah*] meaning "living creatures" is used to describe both animals and humans. To translate the original Hebrew words by "living soul" in one passage and "living creature" in another is not really correct or consistent. English readers may imagine that two different Hebrew words are being used (which is not the case). Definitely, we don't want to read into the Biblical text an idea about the soul that we might have which, in fact, is not really linked to a proper Biblical understanding at all. This is a practice we definitely want to avoid if at all possible with God's help.

General summary concerning "the heart"

To summarize about "the heart", we can mention and conclude the following:

- "expressing inward contemplation"
- "an organ of pure inward self-consciousness"
- "some feeling or action taking place within man (means humanity here)"
- "the elaboration of a plan or resolution"

"we find almost invariably the heart named, and not the soul." (*ibid.*)

5

"The heart" in the Bible can also mean 'mind', 'inner man', 'will' or 'understanding'

In adding to the above discussion about the heart and soul, we have to also mention the following because "the heart" in the Bible can also refer to the familiar concepts of *"inner man," "will", mind* or *"understanding"* as we moderns think of them and understand them today. Let us review the Biblical evidence that demonstrates this idea. Let us continue with the excellent discussion of this subject in CBTEL as previously mentioned to which we will supplement additional authoritative source material:

"But the heart is not merely the organ of pure inward self-consciousness, but also of all the **functions of perception in general**,[7] so that לב (*'heart'* in Hebrew, *lehv*), in a restricted sense, acquires the signification of *mind* or *understanding*," (*ibid.* pg. 115)

Note some important texts in this regard:
- "Therefore, hear me, you *men of understanding*." (Job 34:10 ESV)
- "Why should a fool have money in his hand to buy wisdom, *when he has no sense?*" (Proverbs 17:16 ESV)
- "Behold, God is mighty, and does not despise any; He is *mighty in strength of understanding.*" (Job 36:5 ESV)
- "I will run in the way of your commandments, when *you enlarge my heart!*" (Psalm 119:32 ESV)

---

[7] This is an exceedingly important comment which we will return to later in this discussion.

There are, though, exceptions to this Biblical fact as the "soul" is also recognized as having perceptive qualities in the Bible:

"The soul is also presented as the subject of perception - '*A soul* without knowledge is not good, and whoever makes haste with his feet misses his way.' (Proverbs 19:2 ESV – Note that I added the *italicized* words "A soul" as the Hebrew language reflects that and even the ESV translators admit the same) (*ibid.*)

It is also understood from the Biblical texts that "the thoughts which influence man (understand '*humanity*') are also called the language and thoughts of the soul." (*ibid.*) Note this text, where we see the words "soul" and "heart" used in the same context:

"My *soul* (Hebrew – נפש, *nephesh*) continually remembers it and is bowed down within me. But this I call to *mind* (לב 'heart' in Hebrew, *lehv*), and therefore I have hope: The steadfast love of the LORD never ceases; his mercies never come to an end; they are new every morning; great is your faithfulness. The LORD is my portion," says my soul (Hebrew – נפש, *nephesh*), therefore I will hope in him." (Lamentations 3:20-24 ESV)

The Bible also says that "the soul is the seat of the imagination (Esther 4:13), the place where counsel is taken (Psalm 13:2). Yet such passages are comparatively few." (*ibid.*)

To conclude, we have provided a final technical discussion (see below[8]), but sum up the matter with the focus of the subject of the "heart" in the Bible by saying:

---

[8] On the other hand, the disposition of mind and passion are as often attributed to the soul as to the heart, according as they are considered either as pervading the whole personality of man, or a disposition governing the whole inner nature of man. It is said in Matthew 26:38, Περίλυπός ἐστιν ἡ ψυχή μου ("*My soul is very sorrowful, …*" ESV); John 12:27, ἡ ψυχή μου τετάρακται ("*Now is my soul troubled. …*" ESV), while in John 16:6, it says ἡ λύπη πεπλήρωκεν ὑμῶν τὴν καρδίαν ("*sorrow has filled your heart.*" ESV) compare Romans 9:2; 16:1; II Corinthians 2:4 θλίψεως καὶ συνοχῆς καρδίας ("affliction and anguish of heart …" ESV). We find also grief and care, fear and terror, joy and confidence, etc. attributed indifferently to the heart or to the soul in the O.T. (see Deuteronomy 28:65; Proverbs 12:25; Ecclesiastes 9:10; Jeremiah 15:16; I Samuel 2:1; Psalm 28:7; Exodus 23:9; (where Luther translates נפש by *heart*); Psalms 6:4; 42:6,7; Isaiah 61:10; Psalms 62:2; 131:2; 116:7). Custom has here established arbitrary distinction between the different

"All the impulses by which human actions are governed (see Exodus 35:5, 22, 29), the disposition of mind which regulates them, the wishes, desires, etc., originate in the heart (compare Ezekiel 9:21; 20:16; 33:31; Deuteronomy 9:16; Job 31:7,9,27; Psalm 116:18; Proverbs 6:25; Matthew 5:28); but as soon as the disposition of the will turns to an outward manifestation of the desires, the נפש or ψυχή ('soul' in Hebrew, *nephesh* and Greek, *psuche*, respectively) comes into play." (*ibid*.)

In addition, it is important to supplement this discussion with some further comments from an additional authoritative source. Here *The New Brown-Driver-Briggs-Gesenius Hebrew English Lexicon* is very helpful in this regard. This is because it gives an excellent summary of the various ranges of meaning (that we want to understand) that we find in the Bible texts where the words in particular we are discussing here are used in multiple construct forms providing many different meanings which are all totally relevant to our present discussion. These understandings will also assist us in more properly interpreting New Testament quotations which refer to texts from the Hebrew Bible.

Under the headings, לבב (Hebrew: *lehvahv*) and לב (Hebrew: *lehv*) [pages 523-525], we find numerous explanations of many Biblical phrases which we need to better understand what they mean relative to what is being discussed. This is because all believers deserve and need to have good access to the accurate Biblical meanings as best as possible to help them best evaluate the Bible texts and their true meanings.

---

expressions; thus מרר ("*to be contentious or rebellious*" - biblehub.com/hebrew/4784.htm) and its derivatives are generally connected with נפש (*soul* in Hebrew) and שמה (*joy* in Hebrew) and its derivatives with לב (*heart* in Hebrew). The passage Proverbs 14:10 is of especial interest in this regard. ("*The heart knows its own bitterness, and no stranger shares its joy.*" Proverbs 14:10 ESV) On the contrary, we find נפש (soul in Hebrew) instead of לב when speaking of those functions in which the subject is apprehended as acting on an object. A remarkable passage in this sense is found in Jeremiah 4:19 ("*My anguish, my anguish! I writhe in pain! Oh the walls of my heart (לִבִּי)! My heart (לִבִּי) is beating wildly; I cannot keep silent, for I (נַפְשִׁי) hear the sound of the trumpet, the alarm of war.*" Jeremiah 4:19 ESV) in an entirely different sense we find שמע לב ("understanding heart"), I Kings 3:9 ("*Give your servant therefore an understanding mind to govern your people, that I may discern between good and evil, for who is able to govern this your great people?*" 1 Kings 3:9 ESV) Here we must, however, notice that, as Delitzsch (p.162) very correctly remarks, in the conception of נפש (soul in Hebrew) ψυχή (soul in Greek), the idea of desire is evidently prevalent over all others." (*ibid*. pg. 115)

To begin, it is important to mention that sometimes we find the word "heart" not connected to the human experience at all. We find several passages where Hebrew words appear together with, for example, לבב (Hebrew: *lehvahv*) and לב (Hebrew: *lehv*) meaning "*the inner, middle or central part.*" (*ibid.* p.523) Note the following:

- בלבב ימים – "*in the midst of the seas*" – Jonah 2:3 (Hebrew: *beleh-vahv yammim*)
- עד לב השמים – "*unto the midst of heaven*" – Deut. 4:11 (Heb.: '*ad lehv shahmayyim*)

We also see this same word used in a sense of contrast comparing the inner person with the outer saying:

- כלה שארי ולבבי (Hebrew: *kalah seeri ulehvahvi*)– "*my flesh and my heart (soul) doth fail)*" – Psalm 73:26 (*ibid.*)

These above mentioned examples are fairly few compared to the more prevalent meanings of לבב (Hebrew: *lehvahv*) (heart, mind, inner man, thought). A very important formulation which is found many times in Scripture is as follows:

- בכל לבבך ובכל נפשך (Hebrew: *bekol lehvavhka ubekol naphshekha*)– "*with all the heart and all the soul*" – Deut. 4:29; 6:5; 10:12; 11:13; 13:4; 26:16; 30:2,6,10; Josh. 22:5; 23:14; I Kings 2:4; 8:48; 2 Kings 23:25; 2 Chron. 15:13: 34:31 … " (*ibid.*)

This particular group of texts bears more discussion because we can see that the translation "the heart" really often refers to "the mind" directly. Let us review Deut. 6:5-7 (ESV) (we referred to this text above) in this regard where this is made clear:

"You shall love the Lord your God with all **your heart** and with all **your soul** and with all your might. And these words that I command you today shall be on your heart. You shall teach them diligently to your children, and shall talk of them when you sit in your house, and when you walk by the way, and when you lie down, and when you rise."

What we can see in this text is that the phrase "the heart" is not really precisely definitive, because we do not use our "heart" to take the Word of God into ourselves. We use our minds! We also understand that we have to teach the Words of God to our children. We do this through the agency of and through the use of our minds or our intellects. Sticking with the term "heart" in this text is fine as long as we understand the meaning is "mind". The same can be said for many other such passages.

We can also say the same thing about the following texts which include the Hebrew phrase "אשר בלבבך" (Hebrew: *asher belehvavkha*) (*what is in the heart [mind]*). These texts are: Deut. 8:2; I Sam. 9:19; 14:7; 2 Sam. 7:3; II Kings 10:30; II Chron. 32:31; (*ibid.*) In these texts "mind" is the more correct translation than the "heart".

Another text which is also helpful for us to understand is one that connects other activities with those of the mind. For example, note Deut. 8:5, which urges us to "Know then in your heart …" (NRSV). The Lexicon shows that this text is composed using the Hebrew formulation "עם לבבך" (Hebrew: *'geem lehvavekha*) (*with the heart*) [*mind*]. (*ibid.*) We can see that we do not know something that God wishes us to understand "in our hearts", but rather we know it through the use of our minds, our intellects, our literate thought processes. To know using your mind means that you have thought about the matter at hand. This idea of the text saying: "Think about it" or "Consider in your mind" really better reflects what this text is teaching us.

Another text which shows the action of the mind is Psalm 77:6, which says:

"I commune with my heart in the night; I meditate and search my spirit:" (NRSV)

The Hebrew construction "עם לבבי" (Hebrew: *'geem lehvavi*) (*with my heart [mind]*) is once again used here so numerous translations point out that the writer is meditating or communing with his own heart or more accurately **his own mind**. What is taking place here is a literate activity. It involves thoughts and words coming from the mind. It may not be audible, but it involves communication using words or speech. It is definitely not some kind of a feeling, impulse, inspiration or an intuitive experience.

We also see this Hebrew construction "עם לבב" (Hebrew: *'geem lehvahv*) (*with the heart* [*mind*]) meaning "of a thought or purpose," (*ibid.* p. 523) In this regard, we will refer to a few passages. Note first, Deuteronomy 15:9 (ESV)

"Take care lest there be an unworthy thought **in your heart** and you say, 'The seventh year, the year of release is near,' and your eye look grudgingly on your poor brother and you give him nothing, and he cry to the LORD against you, and you be guilty of sin."

The above mentioned text is so interesting because it again uses this "עם לבב" (Hebrew: *'geem lehvahv*) (*with the heart* [*mind*]) formulation and in this case, the meaning of "mind" is very clear. A better translation of the first part of the verse that concerns us is: "*Be careful not to have an evil thought* **in your mind**." (NIRV)

Another passage along the same line, with a focus on the "purpose" element is:

"Now it was in the heart of David my father to build a house for the name of the Lord, the God of Israel. But the Lord said to David my father, 'Whereas it was in your heart to build a house for my name, you did well that it was in your heart." (I Kings 8:17, 18 ESV)

We see in this text that King David had "purposed" to build the Temple. He "planned" for and "prepared" for this building project. This is the same word construction "עם לבב" (Hebrew: *'geem lehvahv*) (*with the heart* [*mind*]) with the past tense "to be" verb added.

In addition to these important constructions, which importantly provide us deeper meanings beyond the more non-definitive "heart", it is essential to review some further constructions of לבב (Hebrew: *lehvahv*) which really help us to enrich our understanding of the subject of "the heart". A number of texts point out more direct, individual characteristics of the mind. We can note some of these in summary form:

- "Therefore, hear me, **you who have sense**, …" (Job 34:10 NRSV) (Hebrew: *anshe lehvahv*, אנשי לבב – "*men of mind*" – Being spoken to men.) (*ibid.* p. 523)
- "**But I have understanding** as well as you; … (Job 12:3 NRSV) (Hebrew: *gam li lehvahv*, גם לי לבב –"*I also have a mind*"
- "and madness is **in their hearts** while they live, … (Ecclesiastes 9:3) (Hebrew: *wehowlelohvt bilvahvahm* והוללות בלבבם) "*and madness is in (their) mind*"
- "**Dull the minds** of these people; deafen their ears and blind their eyes; otherwise they might see with their eyes and hear with their ears, **understand with their minds**, turn back, and be healed." (Isaiah 6:10 Holman Christian Standard Bible) – (Hebrew: *hashmen lehv*, השמן לב – "*Make dull the mind*"; Hebrew: *ulehvahvoh yavin*, ולבבו יבין – "*and with their mind understand*")
- "But this is not what he intends, and this is not what he thinks **in his mind**; but it is **in his mind** to destroy, …" (Isa. 10:7 ISV) (Hebrew: *ulehvahvoh lo ken yaghshov*, ולבבו לא כן יחשב – "*and this is not what he thinks in his mind*"; Hebrew: כי להשמיד בלבבו - "*but it is in his mind to destroy.*")
- "So teach us to number our days that we may get a **heart of wisdom.**" (Psa. 90:12 ESV) – (Hebrew: *lehvahv chachmah*, לבב חכמה – "*mind of wisdom*" (*ibid.*) or "a wise mind".
- "Let none of you think evil **in your heart** against your neighbor … (Zechariah 8:17 NKJV) – (Hebrew: *al tachshvu bilvavchem*, אל תחשבו בלבבכם – "*do not think in your mind*") – This is a very important text because many translations often use the words "devise, plan, plot, etc.), but the Hebrew root/word means "think" (*thinking, reflection – ibid.*), so the text tells us not even to "*think in our minds*" evil against our neighbors much less "devise, plan, plot, etc.". All of this takes place in the mind with the actions of our intellect.
- I Chronicles 29:18,19 – "O Lord, God of Abraham, Isaac, and Israel, our fathers, keep forever such **purposes and thoughts in the minds** of Your people, and direct their hearts toward You; and give to my son Solomon a perfect heart to keep Your commandments, Your testimonies, and Your

statutes, and to do all [that is necessary] to build the temple [for You], for which I have made provision." (Amplified Bible) - (Hebrew: *leyetzer machshevot lehvahv*, ליצר מחשבות לבב" – *"purposes and thoughts in the minds"* (v.18) The Amplified Bible has a really beautiful translation which really captures well the Hebrew meaning here. The Lexicon translates this passage with this rendering saying *"conception of thoughts of mind."* (*ibid.*) As this is the meaning here, we must comment on some other parts of this text which use the same wording and have the same meaning. Note the end of v.18, which says: *"direct their hearts toward You."* (Hebrew: *wehaken levahvam elekah*, והכן לבבם אליך). This is the same word for "hearts" as found in the earlier part of the verse, so we need to translate this also as "minds." In addition, we see a definite continuation of this idea in v.19, which mentions: *"give to my son Solomon a **perfect heart** to keep Your commandments, Your testimonies, and Your statutes …".*[9] Here again, we must follow the train of thought in the passage and translate the word "heart" (לבב - *lehvavh*) by the word **"mind"** because it is through our minds that we learn, know, understand and follow through upon the LORD's "commandments, testimonies and statues." These concepts are literate in nature and as such it is necessary to understand that this passage means "mind" once again. (*ibid.*)

Now that we have seen a fuller discussion and comparison on the "heart" and "soul", it is right that we present the Biblical side of the story about the heart. This story often does not seem to be told by many religious leaders today. Their teachings are often directed towards Christian women and mothers mostly to tell them they need to ignore and not ever trust their "inner most being" at all and its influence in directing their lives. The "heart" does have a side that may lead to wrong behavior. This is not, however, the whole story. The heart does quite a lot right as we all know if we will just think it through. It is capable of wondrous things and possesses unequalled beauty. Note the following Biblical information which makes this clear.

---

[9] (Hebrew: *weleshlomoh beni ten lehvahv shalem lishmor mitzotecha edeotecha wehukkecha*, ולשלמה בני תן לבב שלם לשמור מצותיך עדותיך וחקיך

"Therefore, also man (better read 'humanity') is designated according to his heart in all that relates to habitual moral qualities. Thus we read of:

- 'a wise heart' (I Kings 5:12; Proverbs 10:8)
- 'a pure heart' (Psalm 41:12; Matthew 5:8; I Timothy 1:5; II Timothy 2:22)
- 'an upright and righteous heart' (Genesis 20:5,6; Psalms 11:2; 78:72; 51:2)
- 'a single heart' (Ephesians 5:5; Colossians 3:22)
- 'a pious and good heart' (Luke 8:15)
- 'a lowly (or humble) heart' (Matthew 11:29)[10]

What? "Habitual moral qualities" are positive and they are found in the heart? Why is this never mentioned? Why are these texts never taught or so much as even referred to? Why are Christian women and mothers given such a one dimensionally negative view of the heart (and especially their hearts) as if there is nothing else to say or know?

So, it is clear that the issue of the 'heart' in the Bible is not a one dimensional matter with only a negative orientation. In no way! There are positive and beautiful sides to the human heart that we all need to be reminded of. They are just as much a part of God's Word as are the statements about the negative aspects of the heart.

"The heart" in the Bible – Ethical and Religious Significance

In conclusion, we can sum up saying the following about what the Bible teaches us about the subject of the "heart."

"As the heart is the home of the personal life, the workshop where all personal appropriation and elaboration of spiritual things have their seat, it follows that the moral and religious development of man (better to read 'humanity') – in fact, his whole moral personality, is also centered in it. Only that which has entered the heart constitutes possession, having a moral worth, while only that which comes from the

---

[10] In all of these places it would be difficult to introduce נפש (Hebrew: *nephesh*) or ψυχή (Greek: *psuche*) ('soul' in Hebrew and Greek)." (*ibid.* pg. 116)

heart is a moral product. From the nature and contexts of the heart, by a law of natural connection – similar to that which exists between the tree and its fruits (Matt. 12:33[11] ESV) results the individuals course of life as a whole; and from them all his personal acts derive their character and moral signification. Hence, ἐκ καρδίας (Greek: *ek kardias*) – "*out of [the] heart*") is applied to whatever is of a real moral nature in contradistinction from mere outward appearance. (Rom. 6:17[12]; Matt. 15:8[13]; I Tim. 1:5[14]). (*ibid.* pg. 116)

So, it is true that the heart can indeed be the source of extreme wickedness. It is also true that the heart is the source of the exact opposite: extreme righteousness! It is no accident that the qualities of the Holy Spirit are called "fruits." Good hearts can produce good fruit! This is the teaching of our Lord Jesus Christ. This is a message of freedom that we (and especially Christian women and mothers) really need to hear about the heart from all religious leaders and not to focus only on the negative aspects.

"The heart" in the Bible – Conclusions

Now that we have a good understanding of the Biblical information concerning the ideas of heart, soul and mind, we are now better able to consider the subject of mother's intuition. We can know from the LORD that He has created women to have special gifts around their relationships to their children. These gifts are normal, natural, and protective. They come from God. They must be considered holy, righteous, to be nurtured and pursued.

---

[11] "Either make the tree good and its fruit good, or make the tree bad and its fruit bad, for the tree is known by its fruit. You brood of vipers! How can you speak good, when you are evil? For out of the abundance of the heart the mouth speaks. The good person out of his good treasure brings forth good, and the evil person out of his evil treasure brings forth evil. (Matt.12:33-35)
[12] "But thanks be to God, that you who were once slaves of sin have become obedient from the heart to the standard of teaching to which you were committed, ..." (Romans 6:17 ESV)
[13] "This people honors me with their lips, but their heart is far from me; ..." (Matt. 15:8 ESV)
[14] "The aim of our charge is love that issues from a pure heart and a good conscience and a sincere faith." (1 Timothy 1:5 ESV)

6

Gut Feelings: Does The Bible Speak About Them?

We have seen in the preceding chapters a full discussion on the Bible and its teachings surrounding the subjects of the heart, soul and mind. Now we want to open up another question in this inquiry concerning what I am going to call "gut feelings".

These feelings are very much linked closely to the subject matter we are talking about relative to intuition because these "gut feelings" for Christian mothers who have communicated with me are very, very real. These "gut feelings" are one way that has been described to me that intuitive truths are communicated to women. Their reality is just as real and practical as their acquired knowledge which is passed on through verbal or literate means. [While both sexes may have "gut feelings", we are focused here on women's and mother's experience with this phenomenon.]

So, if there is a natural reality of "gut feelings" or in particular "maternal intuition" which is attested by numerous Christian mothers (who have communicated with me at least and many of whose testimonies you find throughout this book), it seems logical that we should find some more specific allusions to this matter in the Bible? I think that most reasonable people would think that God, who is all knowing, may have given us some practical and specific teaching about this subject. While the information on this subject may not be exactly pinpointed in Scripture in modern terms, if we have eyes to see and ears to hear and we are open to God's Word, we may find more on this subject in Scripture than we previously may have thought or realized.

Hearing Christian Mother's Voices: A First Step to Understand "Gut Feelings"

To begin our discussion, let's review what it is that we are talking about in the direct words of some of our Christian sisters who are witnesses to what we are here talking about. They describe "gut feelings" exactly as follows:

- "I would just get an **ache in my chest** or a feeling" (Quotation - Lelia Schott)
- "**gut feeling**" (Anonymous testimony from chapter (CH) 10)
- "It just **felt wrong** to me ..." (Anonymous testimony from CH 10)
- "I **did not listen to my heart** ..." (Anonymous testimony from CH 10)
- "but **something just felt wrong** ... " (Anonymous testimony from CH 10)
- "I have always **felt an almost visceral reaction** at the mention of spanking" (Anonymous testimony from CH 10)

I think these testimonies give us a good idea of what we are talking about. We are speaking about something that is internal, it is something inward and it seems to come from a place in the body which is in the gut or in the middle part of the body in some specific way. I think that most of us will find that this general comment makes sense and provides a good description of what we are here talking about.

Addressing the English Translation Problems:
The Next Step to Understanding "Gut Feelings"

An important section of Scripture that has been discussed in this book is one which really is one of the most fundamental texts to this whole issue of maternal intuition linking it to corporal punishment and the inner person. It is found in Jeremiah 17:9:

"The heart is deceitful above all things, and desperately sick; who can understand it?" (Jeremiah 17:9 ESV)

We are not quoting this text here to review it further, but it is in this text that we want to begin this discussion of the major problem of ambiguous English Bible translations.

When we look at Jeremiah 17 in English there is one word in particular which looks very much out of place and does not really seem connected to the subject matter at hand. It is found in v. 10 saying:

I, the LORD, search the heart, I try the reins, even to give every man according to his ways, and according to the fruit of his doings. (King James Version)

In looking at the context of this section of Jeremiah 17, we note that the subject matter is the heart and mind and how God deals with humanity. However, one word is really out of place. It is the word "**reins**."

The word "**reins**" in this passage leads the reader to imagine that God is somehow testing or trying the reins using some kind of zoological description of a comparative nature showing how He tests mankind. But the idea of humanity having "reins", like are used to control or guide a horse or other domesticated animal, just seems out of place. It seems out of place because it is not only out of place, it is a really poor translation of the Hebrew original which is quite clear and easy to understand in this text if it is studied carefully. In modern English parlance, we don't really have another definition for "reins" when we see this word. We think about leather straps or leashes that are used to control the movement of horses or other such animals.

Scholars are aware of this matter and it is their wisdom that helps us understand why the King James Version (which many of the main study concordances and lexicons rely on) uses this word "reins." Let us consider what CBTEL says concerning this issue of "reins."

"Reins, a name for the kidneys, derived from the Latin, *renes*, and in our English Bible employed in those passages of the Old Testament in which the term for kidneys (Hebrew: כליות, *kelayoth*) is used." (Vol. VII, pg.1020)

So, we have a word introduced into the English text which is a type of English transliteration from Latin, which to the English reader today reading the King James Version (or many other versions) in particular is very confusing and, in fact, hides the real meaning of this and several other passages where this word "reins" is retained.

While this word in Hebrew indeed means "kidneys", we must understand that this word is not restricted to meaning solely "kidneys" at all. In no way! What we are going to find is that what this transliterated word from Latin may be hiding is a very important teaching which may also be very relevant to our present inquiry.

First though, let's return to CBTEL for a moment to expand our understanding of this subject. This word in Hebrew, (כליות, *kelayoth*), definitely has a meaning connected directly to the kidneys and to the internal part of an animal in particular which was considered to the best part of a sacrifice, of which there is considerable discussion concerning in the Old Testament.

"Kidney … the leaf-fat around which was specially to be a burn-offering, significant of its being the richest and most central part of the victim. (Exodus 29:13,22; Leviticus 3:4.10.15; 4:9; 7:4; 8:16,25; 9:10,19; Isaiah 34:3) (Vol. V, pg.74)

So, kidney is indeed an accurate translation of this word. But that is not the only meaning that this word has and here we need further data. Note CBTEL (V, 74.) again:

"Spoken also of the "reins" of a human being, i.e. the inmost soul, which the ancients supposed to be seated in the **viscera** (compare the Homeric φρην (Greek: *phren*), **midriff**, hence mind), both in a physical sense. (Job 16:13; 19:27; Psalm 139:13; Lam. 3:13)"

This definition is further elaborated in the Lexicon commenting on the meaning of the Hebrew word (כליות, *kelayoth*) very beautifully saying:

"**figuratively as seat of emotion and affection** Job 19:27, Proverbs 19:23; Psalm 16:7; 73:21" (*New Brown-Driver-Briggs-Gesenius Hebrew English Lexicon*, (כלה, *kelah*, p. 480)

When we understand this, some of these above referenced passages begin to make beautiful sense and start to point us in the direction of an inward reflection towards "gut feelings." Let us consider some of these passages with more accurate translations. What we are going to discover is a whole new level of understanding of these feelings that we often call "gut feelings" that originate in the innermost parts of our beings.

- "God tests the minds (hearts) and **inner most being** ..." (Psa. 7:9 LEB edits mine)
- "I will bless Yahweh who advises me; yes, at night my **innermost being** instructs me.[15]" (Psalm 16:7 LEB)
- "Prove me, O Yahweh, and test me. Test **my innermost being** and my mind." (Psalm 26:2 LEB with my own addition)
- "When I became embittered and **my innermost being** was wounded," (Psalm 73:21 HCSB)
- "You alone created **my inner being**.[16] You knitted me together inside my mother." (Psalm 139:13 GWT)
- "But O Yahweh of hosts, who judges in righteousness, who tests the **inmost being, and the mind**, let me see your retribution upon them, for to you I have revealed my legal case." (Jeremiah 11:20 LEB)
- "Not only do you plant them, they take root. They grow, but also they produce fruit. You are near in their mouths, but far from their **inmost beings**." (Jeremiah 12:2 LEB)
- "It is I, the Eternal One, who probes the **innermost heart** and examines the **innermost thoughts**. I will compensate each person justly, according to his ways and by what his actions deserve." (Jeremiah 17:10 VOICE)
- "But the Lord of Armies examines the righteous. He sees their **motives and thoughts**." (Jeremiah 20:12 GWT)

---

[15] King David in this Psalm tells us that his innermost being transmits to him from the LORD during the night. It is for this reason that many scholars and commentators have assigned to this word a meaning of "as a seat of emotion or affection." (*ibid.*) When we couple this teaching with Psalm 40:8 also written by King David, we can see that this innermost part of the human being can be a place of knowledge, wisdom and understanding which comes from a divine source.

[16] This text is a particularly relevant one for our discussion here because it indicates that this innermost part of the being of the writer, probably the prophet Jeremiah in this Psalm, was something created, formed or fashioned by God. As the texts in this section indicate, this innermost part of human beings has an ability to teach us, so this really represents a very important text for our present inquiry into "gut feelings" and maternal intuition.

These texts are very helpful for our present inquiry because they help to clear up some misunderstanding about the meanings of certain key words and phrases as well as give us a good foundation on which to build our knowledge and understanding of these "gut feelings" or innermost feelings or thoughts of our beings. We find the Bible speaks about them, so it really makes sense for us to pay attention to these texts.

Having said this, it causes the inquiring Bible student to ask: "What about other texts and other Biblical words which also point to what we are referring here to as "gut feelings?" This is a very reasonable and logical question which makes perfect sense in a number of ways. What we are going to find it that there is more knowledge and understanding to be found in God's Word for those willing to seek it out.

The first point is that all of the abovementioned texts were written by men and while certainly men and women both have these internal seats of emotion or affection, it makes sense for us to look at other texts which also refer to the middle part of the anatomy where between males and females, some obvious differences exist.

When we do this, the information one will find further supports our inquiry herein. The first place to start is with another passage from the book of Psalms:

"I delight to do thy will, O my God: yea, thy law is within my **heart**." (Psalm 40:8 KJV)

When we read this text in the King James Version, we might think on the surface that we are here again encountering the same Hebrew words as we have mentioned previously for heart (לבב or לב – *lehvahv* or *lehv*). But if we were to assume that, we would be wrong. Psalm 40:8 uses an entirely different Hebrew word (מעים – *meh-geem*) which the King James translators translated by the English word "heart."

What is important for our inquiry though is that when we look at what Psalm 40:8 is teaching, we can see once again that this word in Hebrew has a similar meaning to the Hebrew word 'kidneys' (כליות, *kelayoth*) and that meaning can be once again **"innermost being"** as is the case in Psalm 40:8. What the Psalmist (King David is the sole author of the first 72 Psalms) is telling us is that God's Law penetrates into the most innermost part of our beings due to its importance in our spiritual lives.

Here again it is helpful to quote our Lexicon which reinforces this idea of the similarities in meanings among all of these words in Hebrew we are discussing here.

"מעה [which only appears in the Bible in plural - מעים – *meh-geem*] only pl. **internal organs, inward parts (intestines, bowels). belly** ... b. **digestive organs**, but without precision, nearly = **stomach, belly,** ... 2. **Source of procreation** ... 3. **womb,** ... 4. In gen. **inwards, inward part** ... 5. fig. (figurative) **seat of emotions; pity ,,, of God's compassion.**" (*ibid*. pgs. 588-589)

What we are going to find is that once again, we see more evidence for our inquiry about "gut feelings" in the Bible. While the word "bowels" is the predominant English translation for this Hebrew word, this translation only captures in part the various meanings which the Lexicon makes clear from the various Biblical contexts where this word is used. Let us review several texts in this regard to the above noted Biblical facts.

- *"one who will come forth from **your own body**, he shall be your heir" (Gen.15:4NASB)*
- *"Upon You have I relied and been sustained from my birth; You are He who took me from **my mother's womb** ... (Psalm 71:6 Amplified Bible)*
- *"See how my son who came from **my own body** seeks my life. (II Sam. 16:11 NKJV)*
- *"my heart is like wax; it is melted **inside my body**." (Psalm 22:14 MEV)*
- *"'Two nations are in your womb, and two peoples will be separated **from your body**; (Genesis 25:23 MEV)*
- *"Therefore **my inner parts** moan like a lyre for Moab, and **my inmost self**[17] for Kir-hareseth. (Isaiah 16:11 ESV)*
- *"Isn't Ephraim a precious son to me, a delightful child? Whenever I speak against him, I certainly still think about him. Therefore, **my inner being**[18] yearns for him; I will truly have compassion on him. This is the Lord's declaration. (Jeremiah 31:20 CSB)*

---

[17] This word in Hebrew (קרב – *keh-rev*) is also translated "heart" in some English Old Testament versions and we shall discuss it shortly.

- *"stirring of **your inner parts** and your compassion are held back from me."* (Isaiah 63:15 ESV) – See note below concerning Jeremiah 31:20 because this passage is also speaking about the LORD Himself.
- *"**my innermost being** trembled because of him.* (Song of Songs 5:4 NABRE)

What the evidence indicates is that there is very much a Biblical idea of an internal seat of emotion, affection or moral direction which seems very much to be found somewhere in the area of the mid body. This is very much what the ancients believed. There are certainly differences in this regard for men and women, but in general, this idea has a basis in Biblical teachings and more efforts are needed to learn more about it.

To conclude, there is one more Hebrew word, *"keh-rev"* (קרב), which on a number of occasions in the Bible is translated "heart", but has a similar meaning to the words we are here discussing concerning the subject of "gut feelings."

This word has a wide range of meanings linked to the ideas of: "inward part, midst." (*ibid*. pg. 899) It uses this term in a wide range of contexts talking about people and things. For our consideration, however, the most relevant meanings that we wish to focus on once again mean the following:

"2. Of inward part of man; as seat of thought and emotion." (*ibid*. pg. 899)

In addition to this main focus of our line of questioning here, it is important to comment on a number of passages which use this word and speak about women. Let us first review some of these.

- *"Sarah laughed **within herself**, saying, "After I have grown old will I have pleasure, my lord being old also?"* (Genesis 18:12 WEB)
- *"The children struggled together **within her**, and she said, 'If it is thus, why is this happening to me?' So she went to inquire of the Lord."* (Genesis 25:22 ESV)

---

[18] This is also a particularly instructive passage because this is said by the LORD Himself. As human being are created in His image (Genesis 1:27), both male and female, it makes perfect sense that we would also possess this part of our inner most beings.

To finalize this discussion, it is important to note that many Christian mothers and women have been told that there is nothing good inside of them and not to trust their inner feelings or intuitions. Many of these ideas are based on false teachings and mistaken understandings of the Biblical Revelation. What must be understood is that while humanity is indeed suffering under the pains of sin, there is ample evidence that God does implant His spirit or His spiritual influences inside His children and this matter has a strong relevance to the matter of intuition, especially maternal intuition.

It is very important for a complete and fuller understanding to review some specific passages of Scripture in the context of our discussion at the end here talking about the innermost parts of humanity.

In this regard, our further discussion about the Hebrew word "*keh-rev*" (קרב) is very useful. This is because many passages of Scripture use this word or its cognates to show that God has placed, places or will place spiritual powers or influences that come from Him inside human beings, which must be seen to be positive for humanity. This issue is of particular importance and relevance for our current inquiry concerning maternal intuition because intuitive knowing has a direct spiritual element which is positive and beneficial. Knowing that God is Love (I John 4:8,16) and provides for all of us with a view to positive influences, these texts are ones which I believe we must pay close attention to concerning this subject. Let us review several of them now.

- "*Thus declares the Lord who stretches out the heavens, lays the foundation of the earth, and forms the spirit of man **within him**,*[19] *…*" (Zechariah 12:1 NASB)
- "*I will give them a single purpose and put a **new spirit in them**. I will remove their stubborn hearts and give them obedient hearts.*" (Ezekiel 11:19 GWT)
- "*Moreover, I will give you a new heart and* **put a new spirit within you** *…*" (Ezekiel 36:26 Amplified Bible)
- "*And I will put my Spirit* **within you**, *and cause you to walk in my statutes and be careful to obey my rules.*" (Ezekiel 36:27 ESV)

---

[19] The first thing to point out is that God is in charge of man's spiritual nature, faculties and circumstances. God is the one who makes the spiritual reality of humanity possible.

As we see in these texts, God is involved with the formation of the spirit of humanity, in its sustenance and in its future. This is abundantly clear also from numerous New Testament texts which are discussed in other sections of this research study. It is only reasonable that when it comes to the matter of maternal intuition or "gut feelings", which seem very much to be spiritual in nature, God through His Spirit seem very much to have an influence in these matters for men and women, but definitely for mothers when it comes to the care of their children in particular.

Conclusion

We can come to some reasonable, studied conclusions concerning this subject of "gut feelings" and their relevance in Biblical teaching. The following points can be noted:

- The Bible describes the innermost beings of humans which have spiritual elements to them.
- Accurate translations of the original Hebrew and Greek words are essential to ensure that we have the opportunity to properly interpret the Biblical texts.
- The ideas of "mind", "innermost being" and "inward parts" are all definite Biblical teachings.
- There is a proven Biblical basis for intuitive feelings or "gut feelings" that originate in the middle part of the body.

For many Christian mothers, who know all too well about the definite reality of these "gut feelings" and having suppressed them or having been told by some religious authorities that these internal leadings or guides, maternal intuition or gut feelings are not positive, I pray this information provides a welcomed relief knowing that our Lord not only understands this issue, but He is the creator, author and sustainer of these holy intuitive feelings, which Christian mothers should cultivate, rely on and feel totally at peace and at home with.

7

Mothers – You Are Fearfully And Wonderfully Made

We've discussed the heart, soul, mind, inward parts and gut feelings. We know what the Bible teaches on these ideas. We've been able to clarify and hopefully jettison some wrong teachings. We are now willing to approach the heart not only with negativity. We now come to the question about motherly intuition. What else can the Bible teach us?

How can we know more about this spiritual acquisition of truth that mothers experience? This calling which reveals the truth from the spiritual realm? This knowing without scientific evidence? How can we know that it is not something to be held back, afraid of or suppressed? How can we know that it comes from the LORD and that Jesus Christ inspires it, approves of it and gave it to mothers to help them protect their children and families and to know truths which could not be understood another way?

First of all, let us agree and understand what we are not talking about. We are not talking about witchcraft or the occult. It is clear to most Christians, I believe, that the Bible condemns and commands Christians to completely avoid all witchcraft done by men or women. This is not what we are here talking about so I am not even going to enter into a discussion of any kind relative to this subject.

Let's review again what Hasting's said on intuition. (vol. 7, p. 397 - article "Intuitionalism") Now how can we link it to a Christian mother's experience?

"The term 'intuition' (Latin, *intueri* – to look upon) symbolizes the conception that one among the sources of knowledge is the direct and immediate apprehension of truth."

Now, this is important and it is here where I think we need to pay close attention and make sure we move this idea into the Christian context. To do this, we don't have to use any imagination or guess work. Why? Simple. Because we have the Word of God to guide us and to provide us truths from the mind of God which we can rely on and it is in this word "truth", where we can find a comfortable place where the LORD and His Son Jesus Christ and intuition can meet exactly on a practical level.

The Importance of Truth In The Christian Faith And Its Link To Intuition

The idea of 'truth' as a pillar of the Christian faith is well known. Truth permeates the being and character of God, Jesus Christ and the Holy Spirit and also the Word of God itself. Note the following quotation which makes this statement clear:

"In Scripture language, eminently, God is truth; that is, in Him is no fallacy, deception, perverseness, etc. Jesus Christ, being God, is also the truth, and is the true way to God, the true representative, image, character, of the Father. The Holy Spirit is the Spirit of truth, who communicates truth, who maintains the truth in believers, guides them in the truth, and who hates and punished falsehood or lies, even to the death of the transgressor." (Psalm 31:5; John 14:6, 17; Acts 5:3) (CBTEL, Vol. X, pg.569)

One of God's key attributes is the personification of truth. God's Holy Spirit leads Christians to the truth. Our Lord Jesus said to all of us:

"I am the way and the truth and the life." (John 14:6 ESV)

Jesus also said this about the Holy Spirit, which he called "the Spirit of truth":

"I still have many things to say to you, but you cannot bear them now. When the **Spirit of truth** comes, he will guide you into **all the truth**, for he will not speak on his own authority, but whatever he hears he will speak, and he will declare to you the things that are to come. He will glorify me, for he will take what is mine and declare it to you." (John 16:12-14 ESV)

Divinity and truth are linked. It is something fundamental to God's character. As God is so closely linked to the truth, we are called to also seek a close linkage to truth. "Finally, brothers, **whatever is true**, whatever is honorable, whatever is just, whatever is pure, whatever is lovely, whatever is commendable, if there is any excellence, if there is anything worthy of praise, think about these things." (Phil. 4:8 ESV)

Now, a question? Earlier in this paper, I referenced a quotation from Lelia Schott from South Africa who said:

"If I was hanging washing or something I would just get an ache in my chest or a feeling to check on baby and sure enough he/she would be rooting for milk." (rooting here means a reflex whereby babies open their mouths and move their heads and search for their mother's breast to feed – Quoted from Marianne Littejohn and independent midwife from South Africa.)

This quote shows that Lelia came to understand a truth about what her child wanted. She learned this truth which was confirmed as soon as she went to her child. We do not understand exactly what is taking place here on a scientific level, but what we do understand is that from intuition, Lelia understood a truth, something that helps her better care for or protect her child. This truth she learned is a positive and holy thing.

Do we think this case is linked to occult behavior? Hardly! Why? Because what is happening helps a Christian mother better know a truth (her child is hungry and wants to eat) that supports her to care for or protect her child. There is nothing here in this example that anyone could point to that links to any negative aspect of the heart, soul, mind or any other agency. There is nothing false or untruthful happening here. There is no question that what is happening here is holy, godly, upright and blessed and approved by God. No Bible text suggests that what is taking place should not be followed, listened to or cultivated. On the contrary, let us see a Biblical teaching in the next chapter showing how maternal intuition is a gift from God. The LORD gave this gift to mothers to help them be better protectors and care givers to their children.

8

"A lesson about Intuition from a Mother Ostrich"

Is it out of place to start with a discussion on mother's intuition by talking about a mother ostrich? Maybe. The important point to consider, though, is that God speaks to us in the first person in the book of Job and He has something to say if we have "eyes to see" and "ears to hear" it. What He tells us is so simple and very beautiful. The voice of the LORD can help us better understand how He gave mother's a special gift or ability to understand truth in a supernatural way. We only need to listen and trust Him.

What can God's teaching about mother ostriches tell us about intuition and understanding truth? In the following text, the LORD Himself answers this question.

"The wing of the ostrich vibrates joyously, Is she pious, wing and feather?
No, she leaveth her eggs in the earth and broodeth over the dust,
Forgetting that a foot may crush them, She treateth her young ones harshly as if they were not hers; In vain is her labour, without her being distressed.
For Eloah (one of many divine titles for God) hath caused her to forget wisdom, And gave her no share of understanding, At the time when she lasheth herself aloft
She derideth the horse and horsemen." (Job 39:13-18)[20]

To begin discussing this text, we have to make a few comments and to help us better contextualize this information. The first point that has to be made concerns the first verse of this passage and what the commentators say about it. In general, scholars are

---

[20] This translation is of a more scholarly nature by Professor's Keil & Delitzsch in their extraordinarily beautiful commentary on the Hebrew Bible (the Christian Old Testament). In this case, we are quoting from the commentary on Job Vol. II, page 336-37 - The Keil and Delitzsch commentary have a first person witness about their visit to the deserts of Jordan and Arabia confirming the information given. It is amazing scholarship confirming the truths of Scripture. The first hand testimonies of experts on ostrich behavior are really powerful stories.

not 100% sure what this first verse means exactly. One can research this on their own and can see some variation in meaning. I have gone with this more scholarly text.

Some modern scholars tend to focus on a formulation in v.13 which asks if the mother ostrich is "kindly" or "loving." I have no problem with that. We have enough information in the whole text to understand the general sense of what it is teaching regardless if the first verse is not clear in meaning in Hebrew. The point is that mother ostriches are **not** really kind or loving. This fact is made clear in the text.

In this text, God speaks to Job saying that Job knows very little about the workings of God's creation. Here the LORD gives many examples, including this one about mother ostriches showing His knowledge of and supervision over His creation.

The LORD teaches Job using a case study of the mother ostrich. Job could confirm this by his own observation because ostriches lived in the Job's home area.

Now, what can this text teach us about maternal instinct or mother's intuition in humans when the text itself is speaking about the mother ostrich? Very much indeed! Why? Because there is a message that we can extract exactly from this text that God Himself has created the ostrich mother bird to function exactly how she acts (and this is what He told Job) and this is super important! Why? Because God made the mother ostrich, according to the LORD's own words and exact description to be an "unwise" mother and a mother who the LORD has not given "understanding" and who "God has caused her to forget wisdom." An ostrich might "treat her young ones harshly" by her own instinct. She might even step on and "crush" one of her young. She "leaves her eggs in the earth" meaning she does not care for her nest or eggs by instinct.

It might seem strange that a mother would behave this way, but God is teaching Job that He is in charge of creation. He designs His creation according to His own purposes. I, like Job, do not pretend to understand why God has chosen to give the mother ostrich such an instinct, but here is where we can learn something and this relates directly to the subject of maternal intuition in human mothers.

The important thing about this text is that it represents a treatise on zoology and the case study is the mother ostrich. This case study given here in Scripture is particularly important for us today who did not attend this meeting between the LORD and Job. Why? Because we are able to observe the same behaviors among mother ostriches today to confirm if what the LORD says here about them is true or not. And guess what? God knew and knows what He is talking about!

In fact, this is just the question that scholars like Keil and Delitzsch asked in the 19th century. So, to find out, they made trips to the region where Job was from and made direct investigations into the whole matter being referenced in this section of Scripture. Their conclusions show that what the LORD is here teaching us is 100% true.

This gives us great confidence because we can also study other aspects of either human, plant or animal life to learn truths from the LORD about His creation. These, in fact, are the instructions we have received from Him. Note Job 12:7-10 (ESV)

"But ask the beasts, and they will teach you; the birds of the heavens, and they will tell you; or the bushes of the earth, and they will teach you; and the fish of the sea will declare to you. Who among all these does not know that the hand of the LORD has done this? In his hand is the life of every living thing and the breath of all mankind."

Because the message here to human mothers as well is that God has also created you to be exactly who you are, just as you are, and you, yourself, alone, are a perfect creation of God! This you can trust without hesitation or fear.

God created the mother ostrich to be the way she is (aloof, unconcerned, distant and seemingly very unloving). He, in His wisdom, made mothers to have special powers which, in contrast to the ostrich, connect you to your children! This is a message we can extract from this passage: Human mothers don't normally behave like mother ostriches!

To better understand this passage, let's look at a Bible based comparison between human mothers and ostriches.

Characteristics - Mother Ostrich	Characteristics - Human Mother
"she leaveth her eggs in the earth" (Job 39:14 ESV)	God has given you special powers to connect to your child.
"Forgetting that a foot may crush them" (Job 39:14 ESV)	"Can a woman forget her nursing child, that she should have no compassion on the son of her womb? Even these may forget, yet I will not forget you. [This text shows it is possible for a mother to forget her child, but that is considered highly unlikely and not the norm. (Isa. 49:15 ESV)
"She treateth her young ones harshly as if they were not hers;" (Job 39:15 ESV)	Mothers by nature generally exhibit and express deep love and immediate commitments to their children no matter what. See the appendix on the Bear mother. (II Samuel 7:18; Proverbs 17:12; Hosea 13:8)
"In vain is her labour, without her being distressed." (Job 39:16 ESV)	"When a woman is giving birth, she has sorrow because her hour has come, but when she has delivered the baby, she no longer remembers the anguish, for joy that a human being has been born into the world." (John 16:21 ESV)
"For Eloah (one of many divine titles for God) hath caused her to forget wisdom," (Job 39:17 ESV)	God has given mothers wisdom about their children, which they will never forget and they need to nurture and be connected to.
"And gave her no share of understanding," (Job 39:17 ESV)	In contrast to a mother ostrich, most mothers have a big "share of understanding" about their children, which is a gift from God, which He did not provide ostriches by nature but gave by design to human moms.

Here we have to take great care to make sure we really have a studied understanding of these important questions, especially when it comes to issues where there are differences between the genders, which have been made by God by design. We don't want to have a mistaken understanding and apply texts or information to one group wrongly.

This is one of the most powerful texts from the mouth of the LORD Himself I have ever read which has a special message for all of the mothers out there.

You deeply care for your children. You guard them. You protect them. You distress at the thought of any bad happening to your children. Your knowing intuitively, your gentleness, your internal maternal wisdom and understanding, your instinct, these are God's perfect gifts and they are something God has given you and do not let anyone suggest anything different!

The LORD tells us here that He made mother ostriches just a little different than most other mothers in His creation. Ostriches seemingly don't care for their eggs, seemingly treat their young harshly and don't care about their behavior, are unwise and lacking understanding by God's design when it comes to maternal instincts.

Just as God made the mother ostrich to be the way she is, God also made you, dear mother, to be just the way you are, and just like the mother ostrich, you, alone, just as you are, are a perfect creation of God. You are the way you are because God wants it that way and in fact designed it like that based upon His creative priorities and wisdom and knowing what is best for you, your children and family and your place in His creation.

It is perfectly reasonable to say that if you have intuition related to your children; this is exactly how you were made. There is no reason to try to change this, suppress it or do anything other than to cultivate it as long as it leads to truth, holiness and the betterment of your life and the life of your children.

9

"...the one who believes in me will also do the works that I do and, in fact, will do greater works than these"

The title of this chapter comes from the Gospel of John from chapter 14, verse 12. John's Gospel is different from the other three Synoptic Gospels. It is more spiritual. Note the comment in this regard from the early church Father Eusebius, who said:

"But, last of all, John, perceiving that the external facts had been made plain in the Gospel, being urged by his friends, and inspired by the Spirit, composed a spiritual Gospel."[21]

Now, when we are speaking about the subject of intuition, we are definitely entering the realm of the Spirit and our Lord Jesus tells us all, women and men, some very essential teachings which we know are true from Him, but in addition to knowing they are true, we can see evidence of this due to what happened with some of the Apostles after our Lord Jesus returned to heaven as mentioned in Acts 1.

We can see in the actions of, for example, Saints Peter and Paul, who both restored dead people back to physical life. (Acts 9:36-42; 20:7-12) These events mirror exactly the example of our Lord Jesus, who raised at least three people from the dead.

Now, raising someone from the dead (especially the example of Lazarus) is an august miracle and our Lord Jesus promises us that (as we are here discussing):

---

[21] Eusebius, Ecclesiastical History, Book VI, 14.7 – Quoted from the translation by McGiffert - https://www.documentacatholicaomnia.eu/03d/0265-0339,_Eusebius_Caesariensis,_Historia_ecclesiastica_%5BSchaff%5D,_EN.pdf

"Very truly, I tell you, the one who believes in me will also do the works that I do and, in fact, will do greater works than these, because I am going to the Father. I will do whatever you ask in my name, so that the Father may be glorified in the Son. If in my name you ask me for anything, I will do it." (John 14:12-14 NRSV)

We see that the promise of the Lord could be one of doing such a miracle as He did. But our Lord Jesus did other miracles and it is promised that we will not only do the same works that our Lord did, but greater works.

The Knowledge of God: Our Promise from Jesus that He will give it to us

Our Lord Jesus Christ possessed supernatural, divine knowledge and He promises us that we will have similar abilities in the future. But does this mean that we, who have the Spirit of God, should not have some of these potentials now, if the LORD wills it? I think that most people would say that this may very well be the case even now.

A good example of what we are talking about here is very much linked to the question of intuition, which as we are herein suggesting means a "direct and immediate understanding of truth." It concerns the numerous examples in Scripture of our Lord Jesus knowing the thoughts of people who He was speaking with. Note the following Scriptures in this regard:

- "But Jesus, **perceiving their thoughts**, said ..." (Matthew 9:4 NRSV)
- "**He knew what they were thinking** and said ..." (Matt. 12:25 NRSV)
- "At once Jesus **perceived in his spirit that they were discussing these questions among themselves**, and he said to them ..." (Mark 2:8 NRSV)
- "**Even though he knew what they were thinking**, ..." (Luke 6:8 NRSV)
- "But **he knew what they were thinking** and said ..." (Luke 11:17 NRSV)

Now, it is very clear from these passages that our Lord Jesus had extraordinary divine powers and divine knowledge, which must be called supernatural. It is not something which people have under normal circumstances.

Having said this, considering the promises that our Lord Jesus has given to us in John 14:12-14, if the LORD is giving Christian mothers a supernatural gift to better understand a "direct and immediate understanding of truth", it seems very reasonable to me that considering the holy outcome of this activity, it must be considered something that should be fostered, cultivated, encouraged and considered godly and holy.

We know that within the Body of Christ, there are different types of spiritual gifts. This teaching is well attested by St. Paul, who introduced it to the babes in Christ in Corinth. Certainly, if Paul felt the necessity to introduce these matters to such who were very immature in the faith, it makes perfect sense that such a teaching is designed to be understood as a basic and foundational Christian teaching, which is fairly easy to understand. Note how Paul mentioned it in I Corinthians 12:4-11 saying:

"Now there are varieties of gifts, but the same Spirit; and there are varieties of services, but the same Lord; and there are varieties of activities, but it is the same God who activates all of them in everyone. To each is given the manifestation of the Spirit for the common good. To one is given through the Spirit the utterance of wisdom, and to another the utterance of knowledge according to the same Spirit, to another faith by the same Spirit, to another gifts of healing by the one Spirit, to another the working of miracles, to another prophecy, to another the discernment of spirits, to another various kinds of tongues, to another the interpretation of tongues. All these are activated by one and the same Spirit, who allots to each one individually just as the Spirit chooses." (NRSV)

According to the above passage, it shows that spiritual gifts, of which the utterance of knowledge is one, are gifts that originate in the Spirit and are dispersed by God according to how the Spirit chooses (v.11)

Here we can understand that from the Biblical point of view, maternal intuition may not be universally given as a gift from the Spirit to all women equally or even at all. Some could very easily say that they feel or believe they have a greater familiarity with this gift or ability or that they have been allowed, allowed themselves or developed the gift through exercising it (by, for example, having many children or having been taught it from a mother, sister or other female relative or friend) to a greater degree to where they are much more mature in using their intuition and trusting and relying on it more. This seems a reasonable suggestion based on the many contacts that I have had with Christian mothers who confirm the importance of this gift in their lives. Many have told me that they learned of it from other women and that they began to cultivate this gift and become more familiar and comfortable with their intuition. In this regard, there is a wonderful quote from chapter ten from a Christian mother which says: "I think there is a reason that God instructs older WOMEN to teach young women how to love their children."[22]

What is clear, however, is that if we accept that the gift of maternal intuition is a gift from God through His Spirit, we have the absolute authorization from St. Paul to foster, cultivate and develop this gift. He could not be any clearer in this regard saying:

"But strive for the greater gifts. And I will show you a still more excellent way." (I Corinthians 12: 31 NRSV)

In conclusion, I believe that a Christian mother would affirm that having maternal intuition that leads to possessing a "direct and immediate understanding of truth", this has to be considered one of the most important and greatest gifts that God could give to anyone.

---

[22] "Older women likewise are to be reverent in behavior, not slanderers or slaves to much wine. They are to teach what is good, and so train the young women to love their husbands and children ..." (Titus 2:3,4 ESV)

10

In their own words – Christian mothers speak about intuition

I have been blessed to know so many wise women who have taught me wonderful truths over the years. This is especially the case concerning the issue of maternal intuition and how this issue relates to the subject of corporal punishment/spanking.

We have noted in this book the tendency for many Christian mothers not to discuss this subject openly. Many feel isolated and fear being open about this issue because often they do not find support among their families or faith communities.

Fortunately, online forums, blogs and especially Facebook groups have allowed safe outlets for discussion of these subjects and for sharing among Christian mothers about this important subject of maternal intuition.

In this regard, I believe it is really helpful and instructive to let Christian women speak directly about their own experiences concerning this issue. The only way we are going to see this issue coming more out into the open and to be considered something to cultivate, foster and promote is for open discussion and information sharing regarding the practical aspects of maternal intuition to take place. I believe in this regard from a Biblical point of view, this book has laid a reasonable foundation where we can say that maternal intuition is not something cultic, evil or based on witchcraft or something unholy. The Biblical evidence in this regard is substantial. As this is the case, we need now to start to build on this idea and further open up more opportunities for learning and education focusing on the experiences of mature Christian women whose experiences can help those in particular who are new to motherhood and are seeking to feel comfortable in their physical bodies concerning these important matters connected to the maternal heart, soul and mind.

The following testimonies came from a Facebook discussion that took place in October 2019. These quotations are direct quotes from Christian mothers who responded to a call by me to speak out on the subject of maternal intuition concerning the issue of spanking children. The exact question that I posed was:

"Mother's Intuition: Have you ever felt intuitively deep down in your heart that spanking your child is wrong? Let me hear from you if you have ever felt like this."

The following are responses given to this question. They are unedited and are included with the permission of the original writers. I have not included any identifying details, but these responses came from the USA, UK, Canada, Germany, Ireland and South Africa. Of the more than 200 comments, the overwhelming response was that the Christian women had felt intuitively that spanking their children was wrong.

Intuition quotes from a Gentle Parenting Group in response to the question above – October 5 2019

"I had planned to spank my children until my husband popped my daughter on her diapered bottom and I realized I wasn't "ready for that". But I knew as time went by I wasn't "ready for that" because it was never meant to be. Thankfully I was already in tune with my instincts in other areas and so it wasn't such a mind battle."

"Yes. Absolutely. Tho I didn't feel this till I actually had children. Before I was a mother I was certain I would spank and I thot the answer to being a better parent was consistency in all discipline."

"This is why I sought out gentle parenting, even though it was not how I was raised. It just felt wrong to me."

"I knew from human experience as a child, that being spanked was wrong and pled my case for my youngest brother not being spanked (I was 13 when he was born) and my parents agreed after years of spanking the older 6 kids. I meant never to spank my own either. But then I was in a church culture that preached and taught the necessity of it. To my deepest regret I did not listen to my heart with my older kids. I do not know if it is about mother's intuition. I know men who feel strongly that it is wrong, too. I wonder more if it is within human intuition when the culture (social or religious) do not interfere with insidious conditioning."

"Yes!!!!!!! Listening to my intuition, God's grace, and research in a Facebook group is what saved my babies!!!! I'm so thankful I listened to my intuition and not my pastor who insist on keeping a wooden spoon in the diaper bag ☺ (yes this was preached from the pulpit)"

"I did once. My barely verbal sobbing two year old furiously demanded of me "why did you do that?!" I couldn't even begin to answer. Every single one of the things I heard growing up that normalized this felt like the obvious lie that is was."

"My 3 year old said "No Mommy! I'm people! People!" ☹"

"Yes, there was definitely a war between what I thought I knew in my head about God's command to spank and what I felt in my heart when I was spanking my child. I remember being 8 months pregnant with my daughter and wrestling my 19-month-old son to the ground to deliver a spanking and feeling in my heart and spirit that it was so wrong. I actually remember saying to my husband, "If I didn't know God commanded this, I just couldn't do it." My biggest regret is not recognizing the voice of the Holy Spirit and relying instead on the traditions of men that had been presented to me as doctrine my whole life. It took me 7 more years of to come to a place where I knew I had to figure out for myself exactly what the Bible teaches.

"Yes. In fact, I refused to have children until I was certain that my husband and I were in agreement on this issue."

"Definitely! I knew that the feeling of Shame and guilt was not something God planned for me. That's how I knew spanking wasn't for me."

"I decided when I was 6 months pregnant with our first that I wanted to practice respectful parenting. My husband wasn't of the same mind but said we'd do things my way since I'd be the one at home. Around 18 months though he started to see the benefits. We now have two kids and I feel like he and I are mostly of one mind on the topic."

"Yes, but I'd say it was the work of the Holy Spirit. I'd only done hand slaps (or thigh during diaper changes) with my oldest, but something just felt wrong and he certainly didn't respond well to it. He even stopped reacting to it. It didn't go on very long before I started looking for some other way and that's when I found GP [Gentle Parenting]. My husband felt the same way and I had been more dedicated to the "loving spankings" than he was. He never felt comfortable with it even though we both grew up and still thought you had to spank if you were a Christian."

"And like countless other things in Western culture, we're told that intuition is wrong and to do the opposite."

"Absolutely! I remember thinking for a long time that I would spank because it's how I was raised and that was what it would take to be a good parent. The thought in the vast majority of our community was that children who weren't "disciplined" aka spanked, would be unruly brats who would grow into lawless, jerk adults.

I have always had a fairly gentle nature, but I think my journey to gentle parenting truly began when my parents had 2 more children while I was in my teens. I loved them so much. I changed diapers, fed them, played with them and then when they went into their own rooms I would get up to soothe them in the night if I woke up to their cries before our mom did. Once I moved out of the house I would visit them constantly, have them for sleepovers and take them for outings. People referred to me as their second mom. I never spanked them because it "wasn't my place" and I really wouldn't have wanted to anyway. Guess what though? I spent massive amounts of time with them and always found other ways to handle any issues that arose. I cultivated a strong relationship with them built on mutual respect and set reasonable boundaries, so they cooperated with me more often than not. As they grew I soon realized that they were way more inclined to listen to me and cooperate with me than with our parents who were punitive and often resorted to yelling/slinging orders. However, in the back of my mind I did still somewhat believe that their strained interactions were just the nature of the parent/child relationship and I didn't experience the same struggles because I was their sibling, not their parent.

Then at the age of 24 I had my own child. My youngest siblings at that point were 8 and 10. Here I was as a parent and something inside me just totally cringed at the thought of hitting my child. I couldn't even begin to imagine spanking. I remember saying that to someone when my daughter was only a few months old and being told that I just couldn't imagine it because they were a tiny baby. Just wait until they are a couple years old and disobeying or sassing. But I had spent tons of time with my younger siblings and had worked in a daycare for a few years. I knew how kids behaved and never felt the need or desire to hit any of them. I sought out different parenting methods and soon found lots of gentle parenting resources. It just felt like the right approach, so I dove in head first and never looked back. My oldest child is now 4 years old and there has been plenty of "disobeying" and "sassing", but I still cannot begin to imagine ever hitting her. We have a relationship that is very similar to the one I had with my siblings at that age, only even deeper and stronger. I also still have an excellent relationship with my siblings who are now 12 and 14 that is built on trust, connection and shared respect. I have never once regretted taking this approach and have no doubt in my mind now that this is the right choice."

"Definitely. Planned on spanking before children. Something changed the moment I became a mother... There was no way I could spank her and was wresting with what I'd grown up with and what the 'Bible says'. Thankfully my husband felt the same and we found gentle parenting."

"I remember every spanking I ever had as a child, not because of the physical pain but because of how disrespected and sad it made me feel. I never want my little girl to feel that way. It was never really a question that I wouldn't spank. Thankfully my husband is on the same page. I just can't imagine hitting the person who trusts me the most."

"Yes for sure. Logically, I know it is wrong because I don't want to parent by fear. However, even if I believed it was right, emotionally I don't think I could ever make myself hit my child."

"Samuel Martin, yes! These verses and the teaching surrounding them is exactly what suppressed my gut feeling that spanking my children was not right. I was taught that while feelings aren't necessarily evil, they should be the caboose, not the engine. They should never be the guide. "Right feelings will follow right actions." In a conflict between the head and heart you ALWAYS go with the head. Etc.

And it was the misinterpretation of the rod verses in Proverbs, which, coupled with this teaching on the danger of trusting our hearts/feelings that kept me from listening when the Holy Spirit impressed upon me the horror of what I was doing.

In other childcare matters, such as sleep training, scheduling an infant vs. breastfeeding on demand, etc. there was no specific Scripture "commanding" me to override my intuition in caring for my children, so it was much easier to recognize those philosophies for the garbage that they are, and it frustrated me to no end to hear the authors of books on sleep training speak almost derisively of the emotional difficulty a mother might have in hearing her baby cry and not responding. It's hormonal. It's weak. It's to be overcome by strength of will, etc. Yet there is not just an emotional response, but a physiological response to a baby's cry. Such little regard for a woman's natural response to her infant fails to consider that God created and designed women, hormones and feelings and milk let-down reflexes, and all, to RESPOND to their babies.

A final observation, and I mean no insult to the gender as a whole, but most of these books are written by men. Men who have never experienced the rush of oxytocin when a baby suckles. Men whose bodies were not designed to physically carry and nurture life. Men who are psychologists or pastors and who have never studied medicine or the science behind breastfeeding. I think there is a reason that God instructs older WOMEN to teach young women how to love their children.

Yet, in much of church culture, we have silenced women. They ARE permitted to teach other women, but men are still viewed as a surer source of an accurate understanding of Scripture. It saddens me that many men I know might consider opening your book or Clay Clarkson's, seeing your name and credentials, but should L.R. Knost say the very same thing, she would be given less credence. And yet these same men would deny that they treat women as less than equal.

In my opinion the silencing of HALF of the body Christ, the refusal to hear truth from a woman's lips, is a travesty in the church today. And I really don't think it's what God intended in Scripture. Yet, like with the rod verses, we have latched onto a few verses regarding specific women in specific churches in a specific time and culture and have made a doctrine out of male dominance in the home and church--which some even carry over to any position of leadership even outside church. I'm thinking of one man in particular who refused to acknowledge my mother as his principal in a Christian school and would only take direction from the male administrator over her because a woman should not "usurp authority over a man."

I could go on, but this is lengthy already. I just really FEEL ;) that this suppression of a mother's intuition has a lot to do with a belief that men have a corner on truth and on accurate interpretation of Scripture."

"Yes. I have always felt an almost visceral reaction at the mention of spanking, even before I had kids."

"Yes, absolutely! Anytime I've ever *thought* about spanking my child, I've always been stunned by the immediate flood of guilt. Every. Single. Time. It has come down to my frustrations and unchecked emotions making me want to MAKE them OBEY. The desire to spank, in the moment, has never been in love of my children and concern over what's best for them.

And in the opposite direction, in the calm and peaceful moments, when I'm well rested, fed, hydrated, and centered, my child can do the exact same thing he or she did in the previous scenario that caused me to want to spank, but I'm able to calmly, compassionately, and peacefully work through it with them without the slightest thought of physical punishment.

My mother's intuition is absolutely a gift from God, of this I am convinced. No book or professional has ever led me so perfectly to care for my children the way THEY need as well as my intuition has done."

"Yes definitely! It's what led me to this page. I grew up in a pretty abusive (verbally and physically) household with lots of punitive discipline and even though there are some good memories, it really affected me the most out of all the kids. Even so, I thought that's what you do when your kid doesn't listen to you. I kept telling myself that since I only popped my son every once in a while when he really misbehaved it was ok. But I couldn't understand why the guilt would keep me up at night and why I had such a hard time with it and why it kept triggering these awful memories from my childhood. I really thank God for leading me to this group and the resources provided here. I've only just begun to scratch the surface of true gentle parenting and wow do I have so much to learn and grow. It's been kind of tough. But I really want to change and break that cycle and be a better mother. There have been many moments spent praying to God pouring my heart out and crying because I'm still trying to heal from things that went on growing up. I know that gentle parenting is not only what's best for my children, but I feel like it will also be for me. I feel like it will help me heal. There's so much anger and hurt I feel towards my parents sometimes, and I'm working hard to forgive and heal, really need God's help with that. It's been tough since I became a parent to understand how they could've done some of the things they did."

"Totally. I actually asked my husband this last night- he's not against smacking in theory (he thinks it didn't do him any harm) but thankfully he and I are in agreement that we will never smack our girls. I asked him why he had never wanted to do it with our own children and suggested that this is because he knows it's really wrong deep down. It really made him think!"

"We stopped spanking when our then 2 year old would cry and pee himself from the stress of the spanking. It shook me to the core and reawakened the motherly instincts that I had been working hard to suppress in order to be a 'good Christian parent'"

"Definitely!!! I'm having a hard time putting my thoughts into words around this....I've written and deleted a comment 3 times now but I really wish to contribute.

It's like, if I were to choose to spank my kids, I don't think I could ever spank in love. People who say you should spank would say you absolutely could spank in love but I KNOW I would not be able to truthfully spank my kids without any ounce of anger showing. So with that logic (which I'm struggling to describe) spanking would always stem from my sin, never from my love. I FEEL that the two are completely incompatible. Supporters of spanking would say there's something wrong with me.

Anytime I'm acting from the holy spirit within me, I have no desire to punish my children.

I've read books that support spanking to figure out their arguments and they have sections speaking to parents (mainly mothers) who feel they could never spank. The section always talks about being disobedient or not trusting in God or idolizing our children. It's always telling the mother they are at their core wrong and should suppress those thoughts and feelings in order to be obedient to the word of God."

"It always felt wrong...but I rationalized it away by telling myself "it was the right thing to do."

"Me! And when I was super vulnerable (PPA w/#2) I believed a group of Christian women who welcomed me to a parenting group... I ended up spanking 'in a respectful way' and more like swatting not spanking. But it tore me up. Then our oldest started hitting and I told my husband I never felt right but I was so lost and vulnerable... So we promised our oldest we wouldn't spank anymore. And we don't."

"I've seen it mentioned "cross culturally". That is DEFINITELY a cause of why here in the U.S. it is so ingrained to spank.

I lived in Germany for almost 5 years. Spanking is ILLEGAL there. In fact, I didn't even see many Germans yelling at their kids. They have playgrounds in every village. The homes are in villages. Their kindergartens are "play based" --- Germany is Montessori based and I believe where Waldorf originated. The OLDER women encourage the younger mothers to CHERISH their children and "let kids be kids". Messes and activity are NORMAL. not frowned upon. And breastfeeding...sooo publicly normal! I had an older woman sit right next to me while I was feeding my baby uncovered. She stroked his head, and talked to me. Telling me how precious babies are. All while I was feeding him. I mean latched on my boob she was stroking and talking to him! Where in America would that happen and not be seen as creepy??? It is SO DIFFERENT over there. So very different. And that is where my true "intuition" started to have the Holy Spirit take hold of my abusive indoctrination. I say abusive because until I became a parent, I thought I was ok. That what happened to me was normal. Nope. It was abuse. And it is SO VERY hard to correct!!! But I'm trying. I'm trying so hard. And I know when I'm wrong, yet I still do it. Like the apostle Paul speaks of. Which definitely makes it worse."

"After a year of being sober and trying, we became pregnant with our first child. Something changed. Deeply, drastically, beyond anything else I've ever experienced before in my life, upon becoming a mother. Suddenly, I NEEDED God in ways I'd never known or thought was possible. I didn't want to mess this up. I needed him in my marriage, I needed him in my mothering, I needed him in everyday things. But more, I learned a whole new side of, and understanding of…...love. I was also forced to face the demons of my past and sort through them. I had to think upon and work through how I had been raised. I had to realize that I didn't have a family unit around me to help me in my new role of life. It was devastating, heartbreaking, and healing all at the same time.

One huge life changer for me was when I held my baby. I would look at her and I would feel such a huge, breathtaking emotion that I couldn't understand or put into words. All I knew was that I loved this child in greater proportions than I even knew was possible. I felt as though I was going to explode, I had so much going on inside. Finally the dam, that wall of protection I'd built up inside of me to be strong and carry on, broke and the flood burst forth. I broke at the realization of what had been done to me as a child came flooding in with a clarity that made me ache to my core. I wept out of heartbreak for myself as well as for the healing laying in my arms at a chance of a new kind of life. A chance to break the cycle. Tears just poured out of me in a cleansing way and washed away my pain as pure love filled me from within that I never knew existed.

As I looked at this child so small, so helpless, and so dependent on me for her everything, I simply could not imagine ever treating her the way I had been treated. How could THAT be good and right and lovely? It flew in the face of everything I knew about God. Granted, I didn't know much, but I was learning that he wasn't the God I had been taught as a child. He was a God of love, grace, forgiveness, peace, mercy, patience, kindness and goodness.

Oh how God turned my world upside down to bring me to where he needed me to be for just this time of my life. I feel as though I just started living the day I became a mother. Everything else leading up to it was just a practice in messed up life that I never want to go back to. Mothering is simply put, the hardest and most rewarding experience you can ever have. It's also been the single most used tool for God to teach me of himself. That first year I died. I died of self. I died of who I thought I wanted to be. I died of being the kind of mother I thought I was going to be, and I embraced the piece of God inside of me and allowed Him to lead me to be the kind of mother He thought I ought to be."

"A Plea to Mothers" - A Guest Post By Heather Schopp

You are your own, and your child's, biggest advocate and protector--and you were made to be that. Own this, accept it; and never forget it.

We women have been engrained with the thinking that our doctors, preachers, husbands "lead" us and should have the last word. We are told to conform to rules, expectations, routines, schedules set by others who "know best" for us and for our children. We are told we are disobeying God, we are being negligent, we are unwise, we are spoiling and being manipulated by our children, if we do not listen to the "experts" and the "authority."

Here's the thing: God has given us a gift, a voice. He hasn't given to anyone else -- the gift of maternal instinct. When we are told to follow another's advice at the expense of our instincts, we are being told to disregard this God-given gift (....to quench the Holy Spirit).

Years ago I was talking to a mom about her colicky baby. She told me her doctor said to put the baby in her crib, leave her, and let her cry--there was nothing else they could do for her. I did not express outwardly the grief I felt and said "God has given you instincts that He hasn't given to the doctor. I encourage you to consider those as well." she bristled and said tersely "we trust our doctor and do what he says."

It's not about shaming, insulting, denying medical studies and facts, not considering others' opinions or shutting out others' wisdom; it's about trusting that our instincts are valid and worth heeding and following.

...but sometimes it is about a paradigm shift in our thinking, even in our spiritual beliefs, and recognizing the authority and insight God has given us as women; and it may mean acknowledging the times we haven't responded according to our intuition (whether purposefully or not), and apologizing. That can be painful -- has been for me anyway, because I've had to take ownership for the choices I've made that caused pain in my children and I will have to continue to do so.

But children are quick to forgive, and through my apologizing and their forgiving I believe they heal and grow. And so do I.

God is THE expert and THE authority and only He can speak to you through that inner voice. What a gift He has given us--an inner guide and source of strength and wisdom....Use it!!!!

"Mothers - Follow Your Instincts" - A Guest Post by Debbie Davison

It took years for me to realize that my motherly instinct was a gift from God, something to be listened to, not ignored and stifled.

It took many years to slowly awaken to the reality and truth that insights I offered as a mother were more valuable than the latest in child discipline (even those which came from Christian leaders like Dr. Dobson, who I followed) or church leaders.

In addition, much of the counsel I received from my obstetrician and pediatrician about childbirth and nursing was downright wrong.

Fortunately, I followed my instincts on some things. On other issues, like child discipline, however, I followed inaccurate Scriptural interpretations.

For that I am not only deeply grieved, but angered: that hitting children was and is still promoted by many Christian leaders.

Since we are Christ followers, Christians, of all people, should be advocates and protectors of those who are vulnerable, just as He was. This includes children from the moment of conception.

Mothers, if you are told to do something that is cold and harsh to your child, the person telling you, whether a husband, grandparent, physician, or pastor, is very likely wrong.

I implore you to read books by Samuel Martin and Stephanie Cox which address Scriptures quoted by pro spanking advocates.

As a Christian, I believe that Scripture is God given, inspired, and relevant to our daily lives; however, it behooves us to ensure it is being interpreted properly.

History is rife with examples of the misinterpretation and misapplication of God's Word. It is very difficult to revisit a topic like spanking, particularly if the deed is done.

However, it is always appropriate to study God's Word, especially on such an important subject as child rearing.

And it is never too late to either change our behavior or acknowledge that our choices were misguided and wrong and ask forgiveness.

For those of us who have the privilege of being grandparents, it is a precious option."

APPENDIX I

The Bear Mother and the Sacrifice of Jesus Christ

Many people of late have been talking about the book written by Amy Chua "Battle Hymn of the Tiger Mother." I have not read the book yet. I've read the following article though and I thought it might be interesting to offer some ideas on this whole issue. My point of reference in this regard is the Time magazine article found at this link: http://www.time.com/time/nation/article/0,8599,2043313,00.html

I am not sure what Ms. Chua's religious orientation is, but as a Christian, I would like to introduce you to an equally if not more ferocious mother: "the Bear Mother."

Anyone who spends even the most limited amount of time watching nature programs will know that a tiger does not stand a chance in fighting a bear. A bear is much more ferocious and fearful.

So here now is where I am going to get a little Biblical and we are going to talk a little about the ferocious Bear Mother. She is far more ferocious than Amy Chua or any other Tiger Mother ever thought of being.

The Bear Mother

When King David was facing the insurrection of his son Absalom, we read a very interesting passage which described him and curiously it ascribes to him the probable feeling of one "enraged." (II Samuel 17:8) Certainly, if your own son was plotting your murder and to depose you, one would not have the happiest feelings at that moment naturally speaking. Yes David was probably pretty angry (more like devastated and heartbroken as we learn from his later reactions about his loss of Absalom) and one who is "enraged" is compared of all things to being "like a bear robbed of her cubs in the field." (II Samuel 17:8)

Of all the choices to describe an enraged person, the Biblical writer here chose a female bear robbed of her cubs as the most extreme description to describe rage. In the mind of the ancients, in their world view, there was not a more violent expression of rage than that exhibited by a mother bear whose cubs had been taken from her. There is an important teaching here I think for us today. This teaching is not only for mother's, but in this short discussion, I want to focus in on mothers a little bit. This is dedicated to all mother's. Love you mom. And also to my wife and mother of our two children, Sonia, love you darling.

The Bear and the Bible

We have all read the stories in the Bible about bears and some of them are quite interesting. However, let us have no doubt that here in Israel in ancient and even fairly recent times, bears did exist (they are extinct now within the last 150 years). Going back to recent times it is noted that "in the time of the first Crusades these beasts were still numerous and of considerable ferocity; for during the siege of Antioch (in modern day Syria - a short 250 mile journey from Jerusalem), Godfrey of Bouillon, according to Math Paris, slew one in defence of a poor woodcutter, and was himself dangerously wounded in the encounter." (CBTEL [Cyclopedia of Biblical, Theological and Ecclesiastical Literature], vol. 1, pg. 797 – article 'Bear.')

I won't rehearse the many Biblical references to bears, but rest assured that we are talking about "the genus Ursus is being meant in the Hebrew texts…" (*ibid.*)

Note also what is recorded again in CBTEL which is very relevant to our discussion here.

"The sacred writers frequently associate the formidable animal with the king of the forest, as being equally dangerous and destructive: and it is thus that the prophet Amos sets before his countrymen the succession of calamities which under the just judgment of God, was to befall them, declaring that the removal of one would but leave another equally grievous (v.18, 19). Solomon, who had closely studied the character of several individuals of the animal kingdom, compares an unprincipled ruler and wicked ruler to these creatures (Proverbs 28:15). To the fury of the female bear when robbed of her young there are several striking illusions in Scripture (II Samuel 17:8; Proverbs 17:12). The Divine threatening in consequence of the numerous and aggravated iniquities of the kingdom of Israel, as uttered by the prophet Hosea, is thus forcibly expressed: "I will meet them as a bear bereaved of her whelps." (13:8; see Jerome in loc.), which was fulfilled by the invasion of the Assyrians and the complete subversion of the kingdom of Israel. 'The she bear is said to be even more fierce and terrible than the male, especially after she has cubbed, and her furious passions are never more fiercely exhibited than when she is deprived of her young. When she returns to her den and misses the object of her love and care, she becomes almost frantic with rage. Disregarding every consideration of danger to herself, she attacks with great ferocity every animal that comes in her way, and in the bitterness of her heart will dare to attack even a band of armed men. The Russians of Latachatka never venture to fire on a young bear when the mother is near; for if the cub drop, she becomes enraged to a degree little short of madness, and if she gets sight of the enemy will only quit her revenge with her life. A more desperate attempt can scarcely be performed than to carry off her young in her absence. Her scent enables her to track the plunderer; and unless he has reached some place of safety before the infuriated animal overtakes him, his only safety is in dropping one of the cubs and continuing his flight; for the mother, attentive to its safety, carries it home to her den before she renews the pursuit." (Cook's Voyages, iii. 397)." (*ibid.* CBTEL)

Note: This passage is very instructive on a number of levels, but before we address these, I would like to say that the reason that this issue is important to us today, who wish to learn more about God, is that presently, more than at any other time, we can study God's creation in the most intimate of ways down almost even to the very fabric of the universe and life itself: the atomic level. The study of animals and their habits is the same thing. We have today the greatest of ease corroborating the facts herein referenced about bears (or any animal mentioned in Scripture) because we can find hours and hours of documentaries, case studies, stories, can go to zoos and ask questions, etc. about bears (or any other animal almost) to know their habits and whether or not these assertions in the Bible about them are true.

There are a couple of points which this text raises in reference to the Scriptural teachings about bears and in this case mother bears in particular. Note the previous passage, where it mentions that the reason for the mother bears' rage is that she "misses the object of her love and care..." and "Her scent enables her to track the plunderer; and unless he has reached some place of safety before the infuriated animal overtakes him, his only safety is in dropping one of the cubs and continuing his flight; for the mother, attentive to its safety, carries it home to her den before she renews the pursuit."

These highlighted texts are facts of a long observation of the habits of bears going back into the earliest of times reaching even into the Biblical period. But isn't it interesting when we look at this animal and how even God compares Himself to a female bear robbed of her cubs, we see that this animal acts this way for one reason and one reason only: THE POWER AND THE PASSION OF MOTHERLY LOVE.

My cousin Holly commenting on this issue says it so eloquently as only a loving mother could: "I love the image of fierceness with which He [God] will defend us and the sweetness of His parenting style. Not a better model is there?

No human male (including myself here) can ever for a moment hope to understand, appreciate or experience this, but for a mother, it is instinct. I think that most mothers share this ferocious love and passionate care for their children.

Yet, what is even more interesting in getting back to our discussion at hand about Tiger Mothers and Bear Mothers, we start to see some differences. While the Time magazine article paints the Tiger Mother as aggressive (can we say violent?), angry, demanding, harsh, rude, and hostile to her children, I ask you and challenge any person to show me any evidence, written or visual, which shows Bear mothers as being anything other than the most sweet and tender, docile and protective, fun loving and patient, happy and long suffering, etc. with their cubs. Oh yes, Bear mothers are fierce, but that ferocity is rarely if ever directed to their cubs.

We all remember the television series' Gentle Ben and The Life and Times of Grizzly Adams (which was hugely popular when it came out). While these are indeed films and theatrical in nature, they show that bears are capable of exhibiting great love, especially to small children as was the case between Ben and Mark in the first mentioned series. Come on, Ben was real and while he was a trained bear, he was a bear nonetheless. Honestly, you never saw a more loving 800 pound bundle of sweetness.

In fact, most people in general love bears and rightly so because we are generally a caring oriented people and bears in fact exhibit some of the best characteristics of love and caring especially for their offspring.

But, you get on their wrong side, especially when it comes to their offspring. Look out! And rightly so! We can point again to the example of Ben. Many times in those episodes of Gentle Ben, Ben was portrayed as very protective of Mark and coming to his rescue over and over again. Then, in the end, you see Ben in Mark's mom's pantry eating them out of house and home with the most pleasant look on his face eating the honey or peanut butter.

So, now I would like to pose a question to all of us who are moms and dads. While almost all of us are ready to defend our "cubs" with our own lives should anyone or anything attempt to harm them, how many of us follow the bear in being the most sweet and tender, docile and protective, fun loving and patient, happy and long suffering? Is there a lesson here for all of us? Speaking as one very imperfect dad, I know I'll be firing up YouTube and looking for Gentle Ben episodes whenever I want to remind myself of what I need to be doing. Frankly, God knew what He was doing when He designed Ben. In fact, when we see Ben, we get a little glimpse of God Himself as my dear cousin Holly said: fiercely protective/100% sweetness.

There is another point about bears. If the bears used in Gentle Ben or Grizzly Adams are good examples, tame bears at least by nature seem to be very friendly animals. This certainly is how Ben and Mark were on camera in Gentle Ben. It really seems that bears can exhibit real qualities of friendship and I think there is some Bible teaching here if we are willing to see it.

Do we all remember that amazing section of Scripture in John's Gospel starting in chapter 13 going through to 17? Here Almighty God speaks to mankind through Jesus as a father. Remember what He said:

"Philip said to him, "Lord, show us the Father, and it is enough for us." Jesus said to him, "Have I been with you so long, and you still do not know me, Philip? Whoever has seen me has seen the Father." (John 14:8, 9) (ESV)

So, in this section, we have Jesus speaking as a Heavenly "Father" to His children and by extension to all of His children through the secretarial agency of St. John. And what does he say?

"You are my friends if you do what I command you." (John 15:14)

He makes it even stronger saying:

"No longer do I call you servants, for the servant does not know what his master is doing; but I have called you friends, for all that I have heard from my Father I have made known to you." (John 15:15)

Now, here is where we see a little glimpse of God Himself in the instinct or lifestyle of bears. Look at what Jesus also says in this same chapter of John 15:

"Greater love has no one than this, that someone lay down his life for his friends." (15:13)

Here we have something defined by Jesus in a very specific way. He says very clearly that the highest expression of love possible is that one would lay down his life for his friends. When we also realize the Biblical teaching that God Himself is the very exponent of Love, we start to understand that a person or being who is ready to die for his friends is really operating in the realm of the Divine. It is not natural to be willing to die for another person.

Recall the earlier section of this paper where we were rehearsing eyewitness accounts of the reckless abandon that a mother bear exhibits for her cubs when threatened or somehow lost and not under her careful watch:

"When she returns to her den and misses the object of her love and care, she becomes almost frantic with rage. Disregarding every consideration of danger to herself, she attacks with great ferocity every animal that comes in her way, and in the bitterness of her heart will dare to attack even a band of armed men."

I think that when we think about this, we need to understand that the reason Solomon and the other Biblical writers used the example specifically of the bear was to teach us some deep spiritual truth that they saw in action when they observed bears and their actions and perhaps it relates in some way to friendship.

So, God Himself, calls us friends and He sums up the reason for this discussion in John 15 about friendship. The reason that He related this information is;

This is my commandment, that you love one another as I have loved you. (John 15:12) … These things I command you, so that you will love one another. (John 15:17)

So we are commanded to love one another and to be friends.

Now, here we have God, our Father, telling us that He is our friend and He is telling us to love one another. So we are supposed to love everyone. Of course, when we look at the bear, especially the mother bear, she loves her bear cubs more than herself and anything else and I think there is an important teaching here. I think that we who are parents, the first and foremost people we are supposed to love and be friends with are our children!

Our children are not to be our servants, athletes, doctors, lawyers, scholars, performing artists, musicians or business people, No. They are to be the absolute objects of our love and affection and they are to first and fore mostly be our FRIENDS.

Before she died, I was trying really hard to contact the late Yolanda King, one of the children of the late Rev. Dr. Martin Luther King Jr. Sadly, just days before she died an untimely death at age 51, I had just received my first contact with her office in California. I had the chance to see some of the transcripts of Yolanda talking about her "buddy-daddy." I have never forgot the following excerpt because it is a powerful witness and example to a real practitioner of Biblical parenting. God bless you Dr. King for your amazing example of what kind of a dad I aspire to be. Here is a great excerpt. I am quoting it here and you can find it around the web and I have no reason to doubt its authenticity because it is a transcript from a live audio recording given during a radio interview given by Yolanda King in 2005. (http://www.goodradioshows.org/peaceTalksL23-24.html). For those practitioners of parenting based on the "rod", you'll note that you have no supporter in the Rev. Dr. Martin Luther King.

"What do you remember about your father at home when you were young?"

YOLANDA KING: My father was a buddy-daddy. He really spent most of his time with us playing, having fun, doing things that children love to do, which is, of course, play. He didn't believe in spanking kids. Of course, my mother said if he had spent more time with us, he probably would have changed his mind [laughs]. But when he was with us, he really just loved us. Loved on us. And the time was short, but it was quality time. And my dad was really quite a funny man. He was a bit of a cut-up. He was a jokester. He loved to tease, he loved to laugh. He probably could have been quite an athlete as well. He taught me to swim when I was four and taught me how to ride a tricycle and then into a bicycle, and we played basketball and baseball and went to the local amusement park. He and I, the two of us, would ride the dangerous shake-you-up rides, he called them "faith machines." We'd get on them and just have a ball, he was a big kid.

I realize, now, that those were the times - some of the few times - when he really had to let his hair down and relax. So, that playful side of him, which was very much a part of who he was, he shared with us. And I'm thankful for that, because the Martin Luther King, Jr. that I know - the Daddy that I know - was a very different person from Martin Luther King, Jr. that everybody reveres."

Sounds to me like we all can learn something from the Rev. Dr. King? I know I can.

Dr. King was clearly friends with his daughter Yolanda. We can all learn to be better friends with our kids I think just like God wishes to be friends with us and commands us to love each other. It seems like to me that if this is what our Heavenly Father commands, it is probably a pretty good idea if we earthly mothers and fathers do the same thing? Make sense?

Now, Tiger Mothers are not friends with their children as far as I can see if we take the material in the article referenced earlier. Far from it. Maybe I need to read more about them, but anyone who raises their children in the following way is in my view not in any way trying to be their child's friend:

"Her stories of never accepting a grade lower than an A, of insisting on hours of math and spelling drills and piano and violin practice each day (weekends and vacations included), of not allowing playdates or sleepovers or television or computer games or even school plays, for goodness' sake, have left many readers outraged but also defensive."

Read more:
www.time.com/time/nation/article/0,8599,2043313,00.html#ixzz1D1uMwhFM

The above mentioned description makes me physically ill. Give me a Bear Mother any day!

A final message for all of us – Let's agree to keep the Tiger in the cage and let the Bear out more often. I am thinking to print a picture of Mark and Ben and put somewhere in my house where I can be reminded of it and its importance.

There is one final thought which I have to throw out there. We would be enraged at the idea of anyone, anywhere at any time even thinking about laying a finger on our children like a good mommy bear, but isn't it amazing that some of us (I almost said all of us and I am definitely including myself here) become Tiger Mothers or Fathers and often don't extend these same feelings to ourselves when we are the ones who are doing the finger laying or worse. Something to think about.

Finally, and I think rightly, a good place to end is the Good Book where it says:

"But ask the beasts, and they will teach you; the birds of the heavens, and they will tell you; or the bushes of the earth, and they will teach you; and the fish of the sea will declare to you. Who among all these does not know that the hand of the Lord has done this? 10 In his hand is the life of every living thing and the breath of all mankind." (Job 12:7-9) (ESV)

I for one am looking forward very much to that great godly bear hug one day and to playing in His forest when:

"The wolf shall dwell with the lamb, and the leopard shall lie down with the young goat, and the calf and the lion and the fattened calf together; and a little child shall lead them (you and me?). The cow and the bear shall graze; their young shall lie down together; and the lion shall eat straw like the ox. The nursing child shall play over the hole of the cobra, and the weaned child shall put his hand on the adder's den." (Isaiah 11:6-8) (ESV)

In the spirit of Romans 12:17-21 and Job 12:7-9.

Other books by Samuel Martin

Thy Rod and Thy Staff, They Comfort Me: Christians and the Spanking Controversy – Available free here in soft copy – www.biblechild.com or on Amazon in hard copy – https://www.amazon.com/gp/product/0978533909/ref=dbs_a_def_rwt_bibl_vppi_i1

Reviews of the book
Thy Rod and Thy Staff, They Comfort Me: Christians and the Spanking Controversy

"I've had a chance to read through your manuscript and I find it very interesting! I think you've made an important contribution, especially to contextualizing biblical ideas about childrearing. I hope you will find a publisher for this book. I'm sure many others would benefit from learning of your research."

Dr. Dawn Devries, John Newton Thomas Professor of Systematic Theology, Union Theological Seminary, USA and contributor to the ground breaking volume "The Child in Christian Thought" (Eerdmans: 2000)

"This is not an easy read, but it is one any Christian who desires to be true to the Bible in the first instance should take time to read. ... In my view this study is a definitive reading of the biblical texts for Christians and non-Christians alike."

Rev. Alistair McBride, Scots Presbyterian Church – Hamilton, New Zealand (see www.repeal59.blogspot.com - July 25 2006)

"Many thanks for sending me a copy of your book. Since I, like so many, cannot read Hebrew, I found your analysis of language fascinating and persuasive. Your exploration of these complex issues is thorough and convincing"

Dr. Philip Greven, Professor Emeritus, Rutgers University, author of "Spare the Child: The Religious Roots of Punishment and the Psychological Impact of Physical Abuse" (Random House, 1992)

"These and other verses, as well as the overall teaching about disciplining children in the Bible is ably discussed by Jerusalem-based Christian biblical scholar Samuel Martin, who has produced a wonderful book, Thy Rod and Thy Staff They Comfort Me: Christians and the Spanking Controversy, available as a free PDF download here with no cost or obligation. Martin has been joined by a significant number of other informed Christian scholars and commentators who are questioning the both the traditional translation and interpretation of these overly quoted verses from the book of Proverbs. I recommend Martin's work for those biblically oriented folk out there who have wondered about what the Bible really says regarding using corporeal punishment of any kind to discipline children—or for that matter anyone who wants to be more informed on this controversial topic."

Professor James D. Tabor, Chair (2004-2014) of the Department of Religious Studies at the University of North Carolina, where he has taught since 1989. He is currently Professor of ancient Judaism and early Christianity.

"I want to take my hat off to Samuel Martin and say, Thanks!

When I think about Samuel Martin, what comes to mind is a contemporary and contextualized, this-world version of William Wilberforce. He certainly has Wilberforce blood running through his veins. He is a Christian living in Jerusalem with an interest in connecting to the rest of the world in ways that are helpful and strategic about how to live out ones faith. Check his website: samuelmartin.blogspot.com. You will find interesting discussions about various biblical subjects.

In addition to being a blogger, Samuel is an author. I just finished reading his book Thy Rod and Thy Staff They Comfort Me: Christians and the Spanking Controversy. I ordered the book from a California source and had it delivered to a Canadian residence http://www.archivescalifornia.com/. Unlike more academic books that I tend to write, which can often be inaccessible to average readers (!), Samuel Martin does a good job of writing with an easy-to-understand touch. For me the greatest benefit in reading his book was to see how a movement towards an anti-spanking position can be developed through Jewish sources and readings of Scripture (as well as Christian ones). He comes to similar conclusions that I do regarding the spanking controversy but his path through the biblical material is quite different - a fascinating read.

Blogger, author and, most importantly, activist! My third thanks to Samuel is that he has reminded me of my own need to be at least to some extent . . . an activist. He has not done this by way of harassment. No, he has shown me this through his own life and example. He would be happy to know that recently I have broken out of my insulated scholarly circles and actually done a handful of radio interviews. Now that is a stretch for a stuffy, old professor of New Testament. Through his own activist work quite extensive as I have watched from afar he is changing the world one person at a time. He does so often by putting people together in ways that help to bring influence on those who perhaps would otherwise not listen. Samuel has reminded me of something that is easily forgotten in the ivory towers of academia, namely, that ideas only work to the degree that there are people willing to influence (other) people about those ideas. So, on three accounts my hat is off to Samuel Martin - blogger, author and activist." - Professor William Webb

Dr. Bill Webb is Adjunct Professor of Biblical Studies at Tyndale Seminary. He has worked as a pastor, chaplain, and professor over a span of over twenty years. In addition to conference speaking ministry, he has published several articles and books, including Returning Home (Sheffield Press, 1993), Slaves, Women, and Homosexuals (IVP, 2001), Discovering Biblical Equality (two chapters; IVP, 2005), Four Views on Moving from the Bible to Theology (one view and responses; Zondervan, 2009), Corporal Punishment in the Bible: A Redemptive Hermeneutic for Troubling Texts (IVP, 2011).

Other books by Samuel Martin

Thy Rod and Thy Staff, They Comfort Me: Book II – The Book of Hebrews and the Corporal Punishment of Children in the Christian Context – Available on Amazon in hard copy.

https://www.amazon.com/Samuel-Martin/e/B00HP94ZZA/ref=dp_byline_cont_pop_book_1

Reviews of the book Thy Rod and Thy Staff, They Comfort Me: Book II The Book of Hebrews and the Corporal Punishment of Children in the Christian Context

"Samuel Martin does a good job of writing with an easy to understand touch ... He comes to similar conclusions that I do regarding the spanking controversy."

- Professor William Webb, Adjunct Professor of Biblical Studies, Tyndale Seminary, Canada and author of the book "Corporal Punishment in the Bible: A Redemptive Movement Hermeneutic for Troubling Texts" (InterVarsity, 2011)

"I think you present a well-crafted argument."

Pastor Crystal Lutton, author of "Biblical Parenting"

"a very provocative and stimulating perspective of Hebrews."

Clay Clarkson, author of "Heartfelt Discipline: Following God's Path of Life to the Heart of Your Child."

Other books by Samuel Martin

One of the most interesting aspects to the early history of human kind concerns the Biblical data showing that certain individuals are identified as having lived lives reaching up to almost 1,000 years of age. We today look at these Biblical texts and wonder if they are true or if they just represent ancient myths that primitive mankind believed in.

In this new publication, we are going to explore this question with a view to illuminating difficult passages of the Holy Scripture. We believe that the LORD has given us all the information that we need within the Scriptures themselves to answer all the questions that we may have on most subjects. Understanding how the Patriarchs in the Antediluvian Age lived to be so old is no exception.

https://www.amazon.com/Samuel-Martin/e/B00HP94ZZA/ref=dp_byline_cont_pop_book_1

Other books by Samuel Martin

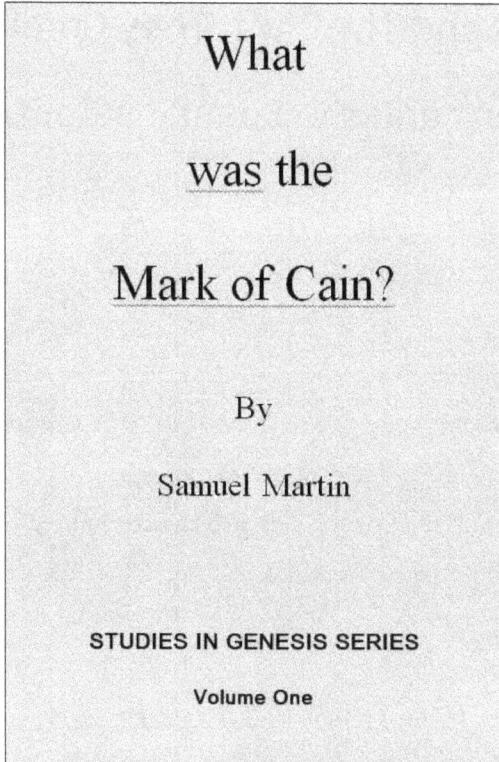

What was the Mark of Cain? Scholars and lay people alike have been asking this question for centuries. In this new book, Samuel Martin proposes a new idea to help answer this age-old question. This new book stresses the following points in seeking to identify what was the Mark of Cain:

- ✓ The early narratives in Genesis cannot be understood properly without an appreciation of the fact that these narratives have very strong symbolic teachings associated with them relating to the Holy Temple
- ✓ Solid comparative studies of the specific texts in Genesis relating to this story with other Biblical passages will pay great dividends in helping to understand what the Mark of Cain was
- ✓ In this book, we propose a number of interesting and thought provoking suggestions about Cain and Abel age's at the time when Abel died
- ✓ A new proposal concerning the Biblical translation of the "Land of Nod."

For information about how to get this hard copy book, write: info@biblechild.com.

Testimonies from Christian moms about the book Thy Rod and Thy Staff, They Comfort Me: Christians and the Spanking Controversy

"Wow! I'm so glad that you have been able to give this book out to so many. [over 400 in the last 12 months] I still am so grateful that I discovered it. It has helped us to parent each of our children with love and respect. We have recently become foster parents and I was so proud to be able to say that we were Christians who don't spank. They make foster parents sign a contract to not spank foster children if they use corporal punishment with their own children. They are so used to Christians spanking there own children and seemed surprised that we didn't. Blessing to you and all the work that you do."

"I would very much appreciate a PDF copy of your book "Thy Rod and Thy Staff, They Comfort Me; Christians and the Spanking Controversy"."

"Well since then I married and brought up two daughters. In the [mentions denomination] culture of the time, under pressure from the ministry, I did apply a limited amount of spanking with my elder daughter for a very few years, but by the time my second daughter was born I had come to the view that this was not a Christian way to bring up a child, and neither daughter was spanked from then on.

My daughters are now two fine, loving adult ladies. My eldest daughter is now married, and has a two year old son, and a three week old daughter.

She too is now concerned to bring up her children in a correct way, but is also aware of some pressure on her to apply spanking, which she has thus far resisted."

"Hello, I am a Christian, expecting my first child in August. I am floored by the willingness of many Christians to twist the Word of God so horribly. I look forward to having this book as a tool to back up what I already believe about parenting with the grace God parents us."

"I am a new mom to a beautiful baby girl and have recently found your blog! I was hoping to get a copy of your book, Thy Rod and Thy Staff, They Comfort Me. I was spanked as a child and always thought that was what God wanted but THANK JESUS for the many revelations I have had recently about parenting! I just feel so genuinely excited about raising my daughter now…thinking God expected / wanted me to hit my kids to teach them right always felt wrong to me but I was prepared to do it because I really believed that to be what God wanted. I'm so grateful my eyes have been opened. And so looking forward to educating myself more on this issue. Thank you for what you do!!! You are a blessing."

"Hello! I am so excited about your book. The biblical spanking issue is one I feel God has put on my heart since childhood, as I was spanked and have vivid memories of it. Where many have forgotten the child's perspective with spankings, I remember them well and with much pain."

"I'd love to read a copy of your book. My husband and I were both abused and while we choose not to spank, we have hit our children in anger in the past. As we have worked on our abuse issues and grown closer to God, it has gotten easier to take a moment and not react out of anger.

Our children's guidance counselor gave a class on Love and Logic and that also really helped.

One of my friends shared your status on Facebook today. I shared it after reading the discussion left in the comments of that status. I thought you'd be interested in what I posted:

This is great. I think it's pretty sad that people are using this status to argue that hitting a child is necessary. How else do you discipline? Consequences, removal, distraction...all depending on the situation and age of the child.

We get disciplined at work and in society without hitting. In fact, we're told hitting and bullying is wrong. Yet we think kids are too stupid to learn without hitting...while being smart enough to understand that hitting from a caregiver is different?"

"I am in full support and am still so extremely thankful for your book. It has given me such resolve and a sense of peace in what I am doing with my daughter. I am indeed treading in new water, as far as my own family is concerned, but I'm also blazing a path to be seen, and hopefully, some day emulated by fellow family, as I go. My family will be the evidence that it can be done by someone with little experience in gentle rearing, but a determination given and confirmed by God Himself. I want to thank you so much for your work. I plan on passing it on to anyone who will listen."

"Yes, thanks. I was tremendously blessed [by your book]. I even went through it with my Pastor, who of course, is old school and is moderately pro-spanking, like most Christians. It challenged him, but did not convince him completely. It's really hard to get through to people who are so ingrained to spanking. But, it did make him think and question many things, so I'm going to continue to work on him, and hopefully the Holy Spirit will enlighten him.

It's amazing to see what a strong-hold "tradition" has on people because exegetically and logically, I don't see the proof for spanking. My Pastor was even a little taken back because he couldn't find exegeses from any of his commentaries on the "spanking" passages. It seems like it's just been taken for granted over all these years. Thanks for you all your hard work!"

About the Author

Samuel Martin was born in England and is the youngest child of Dr. Ernest L. and Helen R. Martin, who are both Americans and natives of the state of Oklahoma.

He lived in the UK for the first seven years of his life before moving to the USA with his family. He lived in the USA until 2001 when he married a native Israeli Christian and relocated to live in Jerusalem, where he currently resides.

He and his wife, Sonia, have two daughters.

His experience with biblical scholarship began at an early age. His father lead a program in conjunction with Hebrew University and the late Professor Benjamin Mazar, where over a five year period, some 450 college students came to work on an archaeological excavation in Jerusalem starting in 1969.

Since that first trip, Samuel has visited Israel on 14 different occasions living more than 19 years of his life in the country. He has toured all areas of Israel as well as worked in several archaeological excavations.

He writes regularly on biblical subjects with a particular interest in children, families, nature, science, the Bible, and gender in the Biblical context. He holds an MA from the University of the Holy Land in Inter-Cultural Studies and the Bible.

Website: www.biblechild.com
Contact: info@biblechild.com
Facebook: https://www.facebook.com/byblechyld/
Blog: www.samuelmartin.blogspot.com
Amazon: https://www.amazon.com/Samuel-Martin/e/B00HP94ZZA/ref=dp_byline_cont_book_1

www.ingramcontent.com/pod-product-compliance
Lightning Source LLC
Chambersburg PA
CBHW031454040426
42444CB00007B/1102